Parakeet book for Keeping, Pros and Cons, Care,
Housing, Diet and Health.

by

Roland Ruthersdale

Table of Contents

Introduction

Of all the birds that are kept as pets, parakeets have been around for the longest and for very good reason. These birds are the perfect size to keep indoors and are extremely intelligent creatures. There are several varieties of parakeets that have been bred over the years and they are among the most visually pleasant birds.

These birds come in a variety of colors that makes them even more popular as pets. With the increase in their demand, these birds have also caught the interest of breeders who create the most spectacular hybrids that you can keep as pets.

If you plan to bring parakeets home as pets, you need to learn as much as you can about them. You will be surprised to know how much these birds have to offer as pets and how complex they really are as beings. They are extremely intelligent with a great ability to analyze. They form extremely strong bonds with their owners and families, making them the perfect companion pets.

For beginners, it is a challenge to have a parakeet at home. It is not enough to just find great housing and provide these birds with pellets and food. You need to make sure that your parakeet is mentally stimulated and gets enough attention from you. This is important for their well-being. When deprived of attention and enough exercise and mental stimulation, these birds develop behavioral issues that can even be hazardous. They also develop health issues which are quite hard to treat.

The good news is that you can learn how to take care of these birds and will actually find it quite pleasurable to spend your time with them. They can be trained to perform several tricks and are entertaining to watch as well. Of course, they love cuddles and playtime for the most part.

This book aims to introduce you to the wonderful world of parakeets. It gives you all the details that you need from choosing a reliable source to get your bird from, helping the bird settle into your home and also learn about different ways you can bond with your parakeet.

The idea is to help you understand your responsibilities towards your parakeet. This will also tell you if the parakeet is the ideal pet for you. The book brings to you the pros and cons of having parakeets at home. The tips and the facts provided in this book are the result of discussions with several parakeet owners. Extensive research to ensure that you get all the right facts also makes this book a reliable source for all the information that you need about your bird.

Make sure that you have the time and the financial capabilities to bring a parakeet home. When you are certain that you can provide for the well being of your possible new pet, you can begin your journey, which will be nothing less than exciting.

Chapter 1: Introduction to Parakeets

Parakeets make wonderful pets for a lot of reasons. These birds are perfect for the urban set up because of their size. They are also very entertaining and make engaging pets.

Learning about the history and the natural habits of these birds is essential for owners to give them a healthy and happy life. The more you know about these birds, the easier it is to mimic their natural requirements even in captivity, ensuring that they are not deprived of anything.

This chapter tells you all you need to know about the anatomy, natural behavior and habits of these birds.

1. Physical appearance

When you talk about parakeets, most people relate to the Budgerigar or the small budgie parakeet. Although this is the most commonly found parakeet, there are over 120 species that are distributed world over.

Each species have a different requirement and the more varieties you are able to recognize, the easier it will be when you finally decide to go out and purchase your own little pet.

That said, they all have several characteristics in common. The most important characteristic that these birds share is that they are all active birds that love to play and will always keep themselves busy.

The term "parakeet" is used to widely distinguish birds that have a small body and a long tail. However, there are several species that can be classified based on several characteristics such as:

- Size: These birds range from small to medium in size. The average size of these birds varies from 7 inches to 18 inches. The length is measured from the head of the bird to the tip of its tail.

- Color: These birds are extremely colorful. The range of colors available depends upon the species entirely. However, one thing that you can be sure of is that these birds tend to have brilliantly colored feathers ranging from oranges and reds, yellows, blues, greens and a lot more.

- Shape: As seen before, the name parakeet denotes a long tail and a slender, short body. These birds have feathers that are tapered. The upper bill has a distinct hook that allows them to climb, eat and even hold on to things. The beak is used by the birds to break seeds, chew and peel their fruits.

  The cere, or the area just above the beak, is usually not feathered. In some cases, there may be some coloration in this region. This is commonly seen in the budgerigar. This coloration is different in males and females and is often used as the distinguishing trait between the two genders.

2. Types of parakeets based on origin
Parakeets are found all over the globe. There are different types of these birds that have originated from different parts of the world. These birds do have certain characteristics based on the origin.

Here is a comprehensive list of different species that originate from various parts of the world.

Australian parakeets

Australia alone is home to over 30 species of parakeets. Some of the most commonly found species of parakeets hail from Australia. These birds are small and have brilliant coloration. Australia is also home to some Rosella parakeets that are among the most beautifully colored birds in the world. Here is a list of the most well-known Australian parakeets:

- Budgerigar
- Cockatiel
- Princess of Wales
- Bourke's parakeet
- Stanley parakeet
- Red rumped parakeet
- Mulga parakeet
- Turquoise parakeet
- Scarlet chested parakeet
- Red winged parakeet
- Blue winged parakeet
- Superb parakeet
- Red capped parakeet
- Elegant parakeet
- Regeant parakeet
- Port Lincoln parakeet
- Mallee ringneck parakeet
- Australian king parakeet
- Golden manteled rosella
- Pennant's parakeet
- Pale-headed rosella

Asian parakeets

Every Asian species of parakeet has its own unique personality. Some of these birds can be extremely talkative while others may never learn to talk. Some are extremely friendly and others are not. It is a common notion that these birds are not as friendly as other parakeet species. However, many owners claim to have forged wonderful relationships with their parakeets. Here is a list of Asian parakeet species:

- Ringneck parakeet or Indian Ringneck
- Derrbyan parakeet
- Mustached parakeet
- Plum headed parakeet
- Long-tailed parakeet
- Alexandrine parakeet
- Rothschild's parakeet
- Slaty headed parakeet
- Newton parakeet
- Malabar parakeet
- Mauritius parakeet
- Blyth's parakeet
- Blossom-headed parakeet
- Seychelles parakeet
- Emerald collared parakeet

New Zealand parakeets

There are three main species of parakeets and three subspecies that are commonly found in New Zealand. The neighboring islands around New Zealand are also home to some beautiful species of parakeets. The common New Zealand parakeets are:

- Yellow crowned parakeet
- Red fronted or Kakariri parakeet
- Forbe's yellow fronted parakeet
- Orange fronted or Malherbe's parakeet

Central and South American parakeets

These birds are not as brilliantly colored as the Australian species of parakeets. They are, however, known to make the best pets. Central and South America is also home to some Parakeet species. Here are the common Central and South American species:

- Grey cheeked parakeet
- Barred parakeet
- Monk parakeet
- Orange-chinned parakeet

- Mitred Parakeet
- Black hooded parakeet
- Tui parakeet

3. Most common type of parakeets

There are some species of parakeets that have gained popularity over the years and become household names. These birds are known to make some of the most wonderful pets and will be easily available across the globe if you wish to bring one home.

Budgerigar

- This is the most commonly found parakeet species in the United States.
- These birds grow up to 7 inches long and are available in several colors.
- They have a distinct black, barred pattern on the top of the head. They commonly have green feathers.
- These birds need a lot of attention and will even learn to say several words.

Psittacula parakeets

- These birds are believed to have originated from Asia. Some of them have also been traced back to Africa.
- These birds are known as old world parakeets and include species like the plum headed parakeet, ringneck parakeet and the Alexandrine parakeet.
- Some birds like the Alexandrine parakeet are more independent and do not appreciate being handled too much.
- There are others like the Indian ringneck and the plum-headed parakeet that love to play.
- Most species are susceptible to extreme weather changes.

Monk parakeet

- Also known as Quaker parakeets, these birds gained immense popularity around the 1960s.
- These birds hail from South America and can grow to about 11 inches in length. They are usually grey and green in color.

- They are known to build very elaborate nests. It is for this reason that they are very compulsive with cage maintenance.
- They are known to have a great ability to talk.

Brotogeris parakeet
- Also known as the orange chinned parakeets, these birds are currently crucially endangered.
- These birds hail from South America and tend to grow up to 8 inches in length. The bodies are usually green with color changes restricted to the chin area.
- These birds are extremely energetic and simply love to chatter.
- They make wonderful watch birds and sound a loud alarm when they notice something amiss.
- These birds love to cuddle and spend time with their owners.

Barred parakeets
- These are tiny parakeets that hail from South America. They usually grow only up to 6 inches in length.
- They have a mostly green plumage but have several color mutations because of breeding.
- These birds are quiet and small in size, making them popular pets.
- They can learn to talk and are extremely goofy birds.

No matter what species of parakeet you bring home, you can be assured of nothing but the best in terms of companionship.

4. What is the difference between parrots and parakeets?

People often get confused between parrots and parakeets. The two names are often used interchangeably. However, there are several differences between the two and it is useful for you to know them if you want to bring one home as pets.

This will help you understand what to expect from parrots and parakeets individually. You will also be able to tell if it is a parrot or a parakeet that you really want to bring home.

The order *Psittaciformes* is made of parrots. The term parakeet is used to describe a species of parrots.

Parrots are birds that are extremely intelligent and colorful. It is important to know that the name of the order is 'parrot' and several species under this order are named parrots too. However, scientifically, the order 'parrot' consists of three different superfamilies:

- True parrots or Psittacoidea
- Cockatoos of Cacatuoidea
- New Zealand Parrots or Strogopoidea

Parakeets are small or medium sized birds that are classified under several genera. Since all parakeets are part of the order 'parrot', in scientific terms, parakeets are also parrots.

The word parrot is not only used to describe an order but is also used to name certain species, often leading to a lot of confusion.

A parakeet is normally known as a budge or a budgerigar. It is, in fact, the third most popular pet in the world right after the dog and the cat. These birds are beautifully colored, easy to train and extremely smart.

These birds may be found in sub-tropical and tropical regions. The size of these birds will vary as per the species. They also have the ability to talk and, with some training, can imitate human voice flawlessly.

The ability to talk depends upon the species of parakeets. The common features of these birds include the hooked bill and the colorful feathers.

Here is a quick comparison between the parrot and the parakeet to help you understand the difference completely:

- **Origin of the name**
  Parrot: The word 'parrot' is believed to have originated from a French word *perrot.*
  Parakeet: The origin of the word parakeet is not entirely known. However, it can be traced back to the old French word *paroquet,*

the Spanish word *periquito* or the Italian word *parrocchetto*. The Italian name translates to little wig which denotes the unique plumage on the head of these birds.

- **Varieties**
  Parrot: There are over 372 species of parrots that are divided into 82 genera.
  Parakeet: There are currently 120 species of parakeets along with several subspecies.

- **Common references**
  Parrots: The larger birds are often known as parrots. These birds are usually kept in pairs, owing to their size.
  Parakeets: Usually, the smaller birds are known as parakeets. They are also kept in groups because of their size.

- **Length**
  Parrots: These birds can grow up to 100cm in length.
  Parakeets: These birds can grow up to a maximum of 37cms in length.

- **Weight**
  Parrots: These birds can weigh between 1 to 4 kilograms.
  Parakeets: These birds weigh between 0.03 to 0.04 kilograms.

- **Distinct features**
  Parrots: These birds normally have an upright stance. They also have a characteristic curved bill. They are found in bright shades of grey, yellow, red and green.
  Parakeets: In the wild, these birds are usually green in color. Owing to their popularity, they have been selectively bred, giving rise to several different, vibrant colors.
- **Clutch size**
  Parrot: 1-2 eggs
  Parakeet: 4-6 eggs

- **Lifespan**
  Parrots: These birds are known to live up to 50 years in captivity.

Parakeets: These birds can live up to 20 years in captivity.

- **Vocalization and talking ability**
  Parrots: Parrots tend to have a deeper and harsher voice normally. Some species have very superior talking abilities. One such species is the African Grey parrot.
  Parakeets: These birds tend to be more musical in their vocalization. Most budgies make great singers. They are also known for their amazing talking abilities.

5. History of parakeets

Parakeets are among the oldest species of birds that have been kept as pets. In fact, the Indian Ringneck parakeet was one of the first birds to have been domesticated.

These birds find a valuable place in the history of human civilization. Even the hieroglyphic images made by the Egyptians contain symbols to denote the parakeet. The fact that the Alexandrine parakeet has been named after Alexander the Great tells us a great deal about how far back the relationship between humans and parakeets goes.

It is rather interesting to see how these birds became such a common household name over the years.

Parakeets are known to have originated in Australia. A species of bird called the *Melopsittacus undulatus* has been thriving in the land Down Under for thousands of years.

The native Aborigines of Australia observed these birds that sang beautifully and grew in huge numbers over the plains. The Aborigines noted that these birds usually inhabit grooves of tall Eucalyptus trees. Their nests were often found in tree holes.

These birds were hunted for meat by the Aborigines using their boomerangs. Today, these birds are known as Budgerigars. It is believed that this name originated from an Aborigine phrase which translates to 'good to eat'.

These birds are also referred to as "keets" at times. The name is also believed to have originated form a Latin word which translates to "song parrots that have wavy lines". This refers to the black wavy lines that are found on the green feathers of the bird. This unique pattern helped camouflage the bird in the grasslands.

It was in the year 1838 that John Gould took two of these beautiful birds back to England with him. These birds became quite popular as they were extremely friendly and very easy to breed.

In just a few years after being taken to England, these birds grew in numbers all over Europe. The demand for these birds also led to the capture of these birds in the wild for pet trade.

In order to protect the native species, Australia placed a ban on the trapping and export of these beautiful birds. This ban is in effect even to this day. You can only buy parakeets that have been raised in captivity.

Today, there are close to 8 million parakeets in the USA alone. There are millions more across the globe. These birds are popular because they make the perfect pets for children and the elderly as well. They are quite inexpensive in comparison to other species of birds and are extremely friendly and easy to care for.

Research has revealed that parakeets are, in fact, among the top 5 most intelligent pet bird species.

6. Natural habitat and range

Parakeets are found all over the world, from the tropical climates of Asia to the cold temperatures in Europe. This also means that these birds can thrive in a variety of natural ranges and are quite hardy.

Originally, parakeets were found in the outbacks of Australia. These areas comprise of open scrubs, vast spans of deserts, grass lands and woodlands. The natural habitat of these birds is quite far away from the urban settings that are densely populated.

Unlike most other birds, parakeets do not build any nests. They prefer the cavities found in tree trunks. They usually choose trees like the Eucalyptus tree. These birds are extremely social and it is quite common to find several birds in various cavities of one single tree. These birds tend to stay in colonies or flocks. They are extremely watchful of their flock and will warn the rest of the members about any predators that may be lurking around.

Surviving a hot and dry climate

Next to Antarctica, Australia is considered the second driest continent. They receive very little rain, with the amount of rain varying quite a bit from one region to the other.

For the most part of the year, these birds need to survive on riverbeds that are completely dry. The result of this is that these birds often travel long distances, sometimes as far as 30 miles, in order to find some water and food.

These birds are often seen drinking the dewdrops off the leaves and cleaning themselves using this moisture that is seen on leaves and grass. Following this, the whole flock sets out looking for food. In case there are any new chicks that have just hatched, the adult females stay back in the nests with them. It is then up to the male to forage for the food.

After about a week of the chicks hatching, the female will join the male in the pursuit for food. When they are about 6 weeks old, the chicks are able to forage for food on their own along with the rest of the flock.

Change of habitat based on food availability

Parakeets thrive on grass and it is one of their favorite foods. Their diet includes Tussock's grass, Mitchell's grass, Spinifex and canary grass. These birds also love to eat farm crops like wheat and wild millet.

When the rainy season sets in, these birds search for freshly sprouted grass. Once they have finished all the grass available to them, they move on to a new location. This nomadic lifestyle is quite characteristic of parakeets.

When the dry spells set in, these birds can also thrive without any water for several days. They get the water that is needed for their body from the foods that they eat. During the dry seasons, they normally chew on the leaves and the barks of trees to get the moisture that they need.

During this time, if they do find a large source of water, such as a puddle or a pond, they will gather around it in large numbers.

Feeding in grasslands

When food is available in abundance, parakeets prefer to eat berries. They will be found in areas that have trees or bushes bearing colorful berries. These birds also forage on the ground and are among the few parrot species that show this behavior. For this reason, they are also called the grass parrots.

They will pick spots that have several low bushes laden with berries and also spots where berries fall to the ground from trees. If food is not available in abundance, these birds will also eat small insects. For the most part, they are vegetarian.

Parakeets always live in areas that have tall trees for them to roost in. After they are done foraging and hunting for food, they return to the branches of trees. They are known to chatter and twitter with their mates before bedtime.

7. Natural behavior of parakeets

The social behavior of parakeets is often studied with the same interest as the social behavior of primates and other mammals. These birds have a very complex and rather intriguing social structure that has provided a great deal of information to the scientific world.

With every study conducted on them, several layers to their sophisticated social behavior have been unfolded. They have revealed that these birds have very complex interactions with their flock mates, proving that they are highly intelligent species.

Parakeets have an unusually large brain in comparison to their small bodies. They are capable of advanced cognitive skills, which makes their social behavior very interesting. They are very different from other creatures such as bees and ants that also live in large populations and work together to survive.

These birds have fierce competition and are also capable of forming very dynamic alliances. Their social structure compares to some of the most intelligent species of mammals including primates, whales, dolphins and even lions!

A recent study compared the social behavior of wild and captive Monk parakeets in Argentina and Florida respectively. This study was conducted to test some popular assumptions about the social behavior of these birds.

In the wild, parakeets are often seen flying around in pairs. So, one of the biggest assumptions is that the pair bond forms the basis of their social behavior. Extensive network analysis and field studies revealed that parakeets, especially in a captive set up, preferred to be around one particular bird from the flock or two at the most. In addition to that, they also formed moderate to weak associations with other members of the flock.

This study revealed that these birds rely mostly on the pair bond but also form other relationships within the group. These different associations are very similar to the ones that you will find in group of dolphins, elephants and sea lions.

These studies reveal that parakeets form several positive relationships with their flock mates. However, aggression also plays a major role in setting the social structure for these birds. There are distinct winners and losers in these aggressive matches which set the rank of the individual bird in the flock.

Understanding these various social systems are vital to understanding the behavior of parakeets. This will help in training and also voice learning in these birds. It also shows us how highly evolved these creatures are.

Several species of parakeets have been listed as endangered or threatened by the CITES. Learning their social behavior is a crucial step towards managing the populations of these birds.

Remember, when you bring a parakeet home, you will also become an integral part of their social structure. The more you learn about the dominance rituals of the birds and try to get ahead of them, the more success you will have in training your birds. This understanding will set you off on the right foot when it comes to things like dealing with behavioral problems in your birds, if any.

Chapter 2: Where to Buy Parakeets

The source that you choose to get your parakeet from can determine a lot of things. Primarily, the health of the parakeet depends upon the breeding conditions and the environment of the bird. If the parakeet is raised in unethical conditions, chances are that he will develop serious health issues as well as behavioral issues that can be hard to deal with.

Therefore, you need to be sure that the source that you choose is credible. There are usually three options available for you- a breeder, a pet store and an animal shelter. Each one has its pros and cons that you need to be aware of.

This chapter discusses each source in complete detail.

1. Why parakeets make wonderful pets

There are several reasons why parakeets have become extremely popular globally as pets. If you are looking at bringing one home, here are some perks that you will enjoy as a parakeet owner:

They are perfect for the urban set up

Parakeets do not need as much space as other large birds. They are able to get all the exercise that they need even with a smaller sized cage. They are great for apartments as they do not need a large space.

They are great talkers

Most species of parakeets are great talkers. In fact, some of them are even better at mimicking and learning words than the parrots species that are known for their talking abilities. This includes the Quaker parrots and the African Grey Parrots as well.

Talking to your parakeet every day will help him learn several words. They also have the ability to talk very fast, in a high pitched voice. These birds are also extremely vocal. This includes chirping, clicking and several other sounds that we will discuss in detail in the following chapters.

They are extremely entertaining

Simply give your parakeet enough toys and he will put up a show for you every hour of the day. They love to toss their toys, explore them, talk to reflections and perform several goofy stunts like hanging upside down on the cage bar.

This will keep you entertained all day. They can entertain you with simple things like palm fronds and carrots that they can shred to pieces in minutes.

Extremely interactive birds

Once your bird is hand-tamed, he can be part of everything that you do. Parakeets love to interact and also love a good snuggle from time to time. Your bird will sit on your shoulder for hours once trained. You also tend to make more friends when you have parakeets. You will interact with other parakeet owners and expand your own social circle. Of course, parakeets are great ice breakers.

You will probably begin to eat healthy yourself

When you have a pet parakeet at home, you will have to buy loads of fresh produce to make sure that they get the nutrition that they need. This means that your home will be stocked with loads of fresh fruits and vegetables. Many parakeet owners vouch that having a parakeet at home has improved their lifestyle by leaps and bounds.

They are easier to travel with

These birds need a smaller carrier in comparison to other parrots. So, if you want to plan weekend getaways with your pet bird, it is much easier when you have a pet parakeet at home. There are several motels that are accommodating towards pets. This will make your journey with your bird a lot more exiting.

They are very easy to train

These birds are extremely easy to train. They are highly intelligent birds that are capable of learning several tricks fast. You can get as creative as you want with the training of your parakeet and your bird will surely keep up. They learn to fly through hoops, can be taught to come to you when called, perform somersaults and several other tricks.

The best thing about owning a parakeet is that you have a manageable sized pet that is extremely entertaining. They are extremely loving birds that form strong bonds with their families. This makes them the best possible companions for you.

So, you need to make sure that your bird has a long, happy and healthy life. The first step to this is to ensure that you go to the right sources to bring your bird home.

2. Buying a bird from a breeder

The most important sign of a good breeder is his or her interest in giving the birds a good life. These are the signs that you need to look for when you visit the breeder:

How is the housing of the bird?

Not just Parakeets, any bird requires enough room to be able to spread his wings and fly around a little in his housing area. If you feel like the birds are in a space that is too crammed or too dingy, it shows a lack of interest on the part of the breeder.

Even if it is a mixed aviary with several parakeets, the birds should have enough room to move around freely and just be relaxed. If you see that the birds do not have room to perch or are practically over one another, you need to move on to the next breeder. Not only is this a sign of negligence but is also a warning sign that the birds could be harboring several diseases.

Lastly, check the hygiene of the set up. Are the aviaries too smelly and dirty? Then there are chances that the birds have been exposed to bacteria and fungi that can cause deadly diseases to the bird. The food bowls and water containers should be clean with no traces of feathers or bird poop in them. In addition to that the floor and the bars of the cage should both be free from any dried feces. Any dampness in the cage is a threat to the bird's health and should be taken notice of.

\#

Do the birds look well fed?

This is yet another reason why it is best to go to a breeder who deals especially in parakeets. These birds have a special diet that is rich in fat. If you fail to provide them with this diet, they tend to have poor feather quality and will also be very skinny.

The size of the parakeets makes it very easy to identify a bird that is undernourished. Now, watch the chest of the bird when it is breathing. If you are able to see the sternum and the rib cage very clearly, it is a sign of poor eating. Normally, the sternum is only seen as a faint line running down the center of the chest. If it is prominent, it means that the bird is not well fed.

How is the color of the skin around the eyes?

Normally, parakeets will have a bright yellow patch of skin around the eyes. If the birds are kept outside, the color is brighter. When the birds have been kept inside, the color is a little pale. However, if the color of this skin is whitish, it is a sign of poor health.

Are the birds too noisy?

In the case of parakeets, just good housing and food isn't enough to keep them healthy. These birds are extremely intelligent and require a good amount of mental stimulation. They are also sensitive to negligence and lack of a partner that they can bond with.

A parakeet who is persistent with the screaming is either bored or is simply seeking attention. Both can lead to severe behavior problems in the future.

The behavior is not as much of a problem as the fact that your breeder would allow the birds to feel neglected and unhappy. Then, the breeder is not really interested in what the birds really need.

If you are getting a pair home, do they appear bonded?

There are several breeders who will just sell you two birds claiming that they are a bonded pair. Now, if you bring home birds that are not really bonded, there are chances that one of them will get aggressive and territorial and may even harm the other bird severely.

You must insist on DNA test reports that prove that one is male and the other is female as sexing these birds visually is impossible. Remember, two birds is double the investment. So it does not hurt to be entirely sure.

Once you find that your breeder seems to have a genuine interest in the birds, the next step is to take some measures to ensure that you are investing in the right place:

Ask for a health certificate

All good breeders will provide a health certificate as proof that the bird was in good health when purchased. You will have to get your bird tested by a certified avian vet in order to get a health certificate validated. This health certificate allows you to return the bird to the breeder in case any disease is detected in this test. You also have a 90 day return policy that allows you to exchange the bird or get a full refund if there are any issues with the bird within 90 days of purchase.

Make sure that your bird is tested for Psittacosis. This is one of the leading causes of death in pet parakeets. If your bird has this condition, it can spread it to other birds in your household too. If Psittacosis is detected, most breeders will give your entire money back to you.

Check the history of your breeder's aviary

You can learn more about the aviary from the breeder and his staff. Try to understand if there were any outbreaks of diseases like Parakeet Wasting Disease in the aviary in the past. Most breeders will deny it, of course. That is why you need to do your research by talking to vendors like the food and housing providers or even pet stores that the aviary may be providing specimens for.

In case you do find out about the outbreak from a third source, do not invest on this breeder. However, if the breeder owns up to the outbreak and is able to tell you how they controlled the disease within the aviary, he is certainly trustworthy.

There are several bird clubs who can testify for well-known breeders. You can even look for more information about your breeder's practices in these arenas and forums.

Ask for references

The best people to check up for more information about the breeder are the people who have bought pets from him. Any good breeder will be happy to visit one of his babies with you. If your breeder is hesitant to share this information, it is a sign that something is amiss.

References always work to your advantage in the future. These people will also become valuable contacts to have when you begin your journey with your own parakeet.

Other signs of a trustworthy breeder are a fully functioning website, the ability of his team to work with the birds, his confidence in answering your queries and the general behavior of the individual around these birds. If you see that the breeder is caring and gentle, he may have taken good care of the birds.

Someone who has put in a lot of effort in the bird's wellbeing will also need to be sure that he finds a good home. So, if your breeder asks you a few questions about your schedule and your plans on caring for the bird, it is a good thing. On the other hand, if he is only keen on making a sale, he is probably only commercially inclined.

A knowledgeable breeder along with a good avian vet are very important in your journey with a parakeet. These birds have specific demands in terms of the diet and the ambience that they are kept in. A good breeder will help you with everything that you need as he is genuinely concerned about the well-being of his birds.

Choose handfed birds

If you are a first time buyer, insist on birds that have been handfed only. While it is possible to train parakeets pretty easily considering their intelligence, it is not really a good idea to train the birds after you have brought them into your home if you are a first time owner.

Now, our fingers and hands are pretty intimidating to birds. They also closely resemble branches of the trees or even the worms to most birds. They are likely to take a bite on them or just nibble on your fingers as an attempt to find a suitable perch. With smaller birds, this is acceptable. But if you bring home a juvenile or adult Parakeet, even the slightest friendly nibble can cause some serious damage.

These birds have a very strong biting ability and are known to easily crack the hardest nuts with great ease. Therefore, new owners should look for birds that have been handfed.

When they are younger, hand feeding these birds makes them used to the way our hands move. These birds are comfortable being handled and are less likely to perceive your fingers as a threat. It is also much easier to train these birds.

However, if you want to hand train the birds yourself, it is a good idea to bring home a baby. These birds are smaller and their bite will not hurt you as much. Of course, with younger birds, they are not as easily threatened. They tend to be more welcoming because of their curiosity towards new experiences.

For first time owners, handfed birds are the easier and safer options. If you adopt or want to bring home an adult bird who is not hand tamed, it is a good idea to look for a professional trainer who can help you train the bird.

Buying from an online breeder

Many pet owners believe that buying from an online breeder is actually quite a good idea. It certainly is if the breeder is well known and has a reputation for selling only healthy birds. However, with a bird as expensive as the parakeet, this is not a risk that is worth taking.

Now, you need to understand that with online breeders, you have no way of knowing how the birds have been maintained. There could be several pictures on their website. However, unless you can check the place yourself or can have a friend or family member do that for you, it is advisable not to invest in online purchases.

There is a 50% chance that you will get a beautiful, healthy bird. However the other 50% is a risk that you cannot take with parakeets. Even if you pay half the price of the bird as an advance, it is a good amount of money.

With online breeders, even a reputable one is not advisable for birds like this. You see, after the bird has been shipped, there is not much control that the breeder has over the travelling conditions of the bird.

There are chances that you will get a fatigued bird whose health has been compromised due to lack of food or proper transport conditions.

If you insist on online purchase of a parakeet for convenience purposes, here are a few things that you need to keep in mind:

- Only opt for breeders who can be recommended by friends and family. They should have personally made a purchase for the recommendation to be of value to you.

- Do not choose a breeder who is too far away from your city. It is best to choose someone in a city that you can reach in under 5 hours by flight. If your birds need to spend long hours on the flight, it is not good for his health.

- Ask for a health certificate with your bird. Tests should be based on blood and fecal samples. That helps you ensure that there are no chances of psittacosis in your parakeet.

- Ask your breeders to provide you with contacts of people that he has shipped birds to in the past. Any good breeder will share this information easily.

Of course, with online purchases, scams cannot be neglected. There are several individuals who will try to make a quick buck out of your requirement. Now, when you are looking online, you are going to look in a search engine most probably. This notifies people who run fake websites.

There have been instances when potential owners have received pictures of birds that belong to someone else. In these pictures, you will even see the owner of the bird that these scam websites claim to be themselves.

You can catch a scam pretty easily. They will approach you persistently to make a sale. In addition to that, they will ask you to pay small amounts in intervals. They will keep on adding new expenses like insurance, transport etc. An authorized breeder will know what expenses are involved and will give you a full invoice and costing for transporting the bird.

When a breeder approaches you to make a sale, make sure you ask them questions about parakeets. Ask them about the breeding season of the bird, the diet, the care required etc. These questions should be asked over the phone to make sure that they are not looking for answers online.

Anyone interested in just scamming you will have no idea about these birds most often.

Lastly, you need to ask them for contacts of people that they have already sold birds to. If they are reluctant or do not share this information for any other reason, you need to become aware that they are trying to scam you.

People have lost hundreds of dollars trying to make online purchases. Most of these websites will be pulled down within days of "making a sale" or getting an advance from people. Remember, never pay the full amount to a breeder until you receive the bird in good condition when you are placing an order online.

3. Buying from pet shops
Getting a parakeet from a pet store should be your last option. The reason for this is that these birds do not get the specialized care that they require when they are in a pet store with several other birds and animals, perhaps. However, if you are convinced that a local pet store is known for the quality of parakeets that they sell, here are a few things that you need to keep in mind:

- Make sure that the pet store has a license to sell exotic birds. You can check the CITES website for all the details on the license required to buy and sell exotic birds.

- You need to ensure that these birds are being sourced by local breeders. Since importing these birds is illegal, these birds should be bred in captivity. Find out about the breeder that they deal with in detail.

- Check the ambience that the bird is being raised in. A parakeet is not a commodity that you pick off the shelf even if it is in a slightly messy environment. These birds hate crammed and dirty places. They will develop behavioral problems and could also be carriers of several diseases when kept in such conditions.

- The pet store should provide a health guarantee for the birds that they sell, especially the exotic ones. Insist on this guarantee because parakeets are extremely expensive.

- The bird should look healthy and active. On the other hand, if he or she is lethargic and is afraid of people, it might be a challenge for you to make the bird a part of your family.

- The staff should be interested in the well-being of the bird and should be able to provide you with information regarding the care and maintenance of the bird. If you see that they are negligent and are only trying to make a sale, they have most likely invested almost nothing in the bird's well-being.

4. Adopting a parakeet

If you are a slightly experienced bird owner, you are probably ready to adopt a parakeet. What you need to know about adopting any bird is that you are probably going to find an adult bird that also has a history of abandonment or even abuse. These birds tend to be shy or aggressive, depending upon the experiences that they have had in the past.

With adoption, you need to know that the birds need additional care which you will be able to provide only after you have some experience with the birds. You may also have to spend more money on the medical treatment of these birds in order to bring them back to good health.

Adoption agencies are very particular about the care that the birds are going to receive. Therefore, they have two options for all the birds that come under their care. One is lifetime sanctuary where the birds are kept in the adoption center till they die. This is normally done when the bird requires that kind of attention because of some health issue that it has. In addition to that, when some people give their birds up, they request lifetime care to make sure that the bird is in good hands.

The second option is when the birds are put up for adoption. Now, with the parakeet, they are exceptionally careful about the adoption process, as these birds are highly vulnerable to exploitation for commercial gains.

The adoption process

The first step to adopting a parakeet is to fill out an application form for adoption. This application form will ask for details about your profession, your experience with birds and also the reason for adoption.

Following this application form, you will be asked to take basic lessons about caring for parakeets. These lessons could either be online or offline. You will also be given access to a lot of their educational material that you can refer to after taking the bird home. Many adoption agencies require that you complete a certain number of these basic classes before you are allowed to take a bird home.

After you have completed the required number of training hours, you will be allowed to take a tour of the aviary and the adoption center. That way, you get an idea about all the birds that are available for adoption. There are several cases when people decide that they want a certain bird but end up getting a different species altogether.

The idea is to form a bond with the right bird. Parakeets are birds with large personalities. If your personality does not match the bird's personality, you will have a tough time getting your bird to bond with you and actually want to be around you.

The last thing to do would be to visit the bird of your choice frequently. Once you have made up your mind to take a certain Parakeet home, you need to let the bird get acquainted with you. You will also learn simple things like handling the bird, feeding him and cleaning the cage up etc. from the experts at the adoption agency.

Sometimes, it may so happen that you set your heart and mind on one bird who just does not seem to be interested. It is natural for that to happen. All you need to do is be patient with the bird and visit him as many times as you can.

When you are ready to take the bird home, most of these adoption centers will pay a visit to your home and will take care of all the little details required to help you get the bird settled into your home.

Now, if you already have pet birds at home, you will be required to present a full veterinary test result of each bird. This helps the agency ensure that the bird they are sending to your home does not have any vulnerability to fatal diseases. There are certain health standards that each of these agencies set for the health of your pet bird.

Are there any fees involved?

Most agencies and foundations will charge you an application fee that will include access to educational DVDs, toys and other assistance from the foundation.

You will also have to pay an adoption fee that may go up to $100 for a parakeet. These two separate fees are charged to make sure that you get all the assistance that you need with respect to making a positive start with your parakeet.

In addition to that, most agencies charge a rather high fee to ensure that the individuals who are investing in the bird are genuinely interested in having the bird. These fees will ward off people who want to just take the bird home for free with no clue about its care. Of course, you also need to consider the care provided to these birds while they are under the care of the foundation. These fees cover all of that including the medical requirements of your bird. It is also the only source to pay the dedicated staff who take care of these abandoned or rescued birds day in and day out.

From the time you make the application for a parakeet, it takes about 6-10 weeks for it to be approved and for the bird to be sent to your home. Most of these centers will also have a probationary period of 90 days during which you will have to keep sending records of how the bird is progressing to them. They will also pay home visits to ensure that the bird is being maintained well without any health issues. If the ambience or the facilities provided to the bird are not good enough, the bird will be taken back with no reimbursement of the adoption fee.

5. Transporting the bird to your home

When you bring your bird home, you need to keep the journey from the pet store or the breeders' to your home pleasant. Although pleasant is really not something that you can achieve, you can at least try to ensure that you keep your bird comfortable. Here are a few steps that you need to take:

- Place your birds in a carrier. If you are using a small box for the transfer, make sure that you have enough air holes for the bird to breathe comfortably.

- Drape a towel over the box of the cage to make the bird feel additionally secure due to the effect of darkness.

- You will have to make the floor of the cage or box non-slippery. This will ensure that the bird does not slip around the box as you drive. You may simply place a towel to make this happen for your bird.

- Secure the carrier. If possible, put it in some place where it will not move around. The passenger seat is the best option, as you can also secure it with a seat belt.

During the drive home, you need to ensure that the box or cage is never placed in a crammed space such as the boot of the car or the dashboard. The latter will kill the bird thanks to all the exhaust fumes.

Chapter 3: Once the Parakeet is Home

It is extremely important to make sure that your bird is comfortable from the time he is in your home. The shift to a new environment can be extremely stressful for birds and therefore, you need to ensure that you make appropriate preparations to reduce this stress and keep the bird as calm as possible.

1. Housing

When your bird is home, you need to make sure that he has a temporary shelter at least that has been set up to keep him feeling safe and secure.

Where you place the cage makes all the difference. In case of smaller birds like parakeets, the travel cage and the permanent enclosure can be the same, unless there is an aviary that you want to release the birds into.

If you need transfer your bird from one cage to the other, just keep the door of the travel cage facing the door of the actual enclosure and wait for your bird to take the step into his new home.

Here are a few things that you need to keep in mind when you are setting up the cage of the new bird:

- Make sure that it is in a place that is quiet but still adjacent to all the activities of the family. The bird should be able to see you and your family but should not be in the middle of any commotion.

- The cage should be rested against something to make the bird feel comfortable. The best option is to keep the cage against a wall. That way the bird will never be caught off guard and will not have to worry about someone creeping up on him.

- The bird shouldn't be in for any surprises. That means, any large furniture that may block your bird's view of your home should be accounted for.

- The bird should get enough sunlight but not direct sunlight. Make sure that the cage is not directly in front of a window. This may overheat the bird.

- If the cage is near the window, however, it is a great way for your bird to stay entertained.

- The kitchen is the worst place for a bird cage. The bird may be exposed to several fumes as well as smoke that can be fatal. The fumes from non-stick cookware can be very dangerous.

- You do not have to worry about getting your bird many toys on the first day. In fact, if you are bringing the bird home from the breeder, you may want to take an old toy back to help your bird have some sort of familiarity in the new home.

- Line the cage with enough substrate. On the first day, it is likely that your bird may poop several times making the cage dirty. This is primarily because of the anxiety of being in a new place.

Once you have taken care of all these steps, the rest is up to how you interact with the bird and how the bird perceives you and your family. The time that the bird takes to get accustomed to the new home depends upon each individual bird and the history of the bird's relationship with human beings.

Cage requirements

Number to size ratio

There are a few rules that you need to follow when choosing the size of the cage that you want to keep your bird in. There is a value called the bird number to size ratio. In the case of parakeets, you should be able to provide about 3-4 inches of floor space for every pair of birds that you want to house.

The height of the cage is not really important as it does not really interfere in the personal space of each bird. What is important to note is that the movement of parakeets is mostly horizontal and rarely vertical.

Of course, if your cage is very tall, the birds will like to take the highest perch to rest themselves. This is the only vertical space that the birds will fight for. In general, parakeets will opt for the perches and the vertical space if they do not have ample floor space to move around in.

The ideal size for a cage for your parakeets is 6ft x 2ft x 3ft (length, depth and height). This should be able to accommodate three pairs of birds easily.

Here are some things you must NOT do when you are buying a cage for your parakeets:

- Do not go for enclosures that are too decorative and intricate in design.

- Make sure that the cage does not have many crevices that will be difficult for you to clean in the future.

- Cylindrical cages should be avoided, particularly ones that are small in their diameter.

- There should not be any gaps that may trap the feet of the birds.

- Watch out for paint that may peel off from the cage or from the perches or other items on the cage.

- Do not get any decorative items that use treated wood as they may harm the bird.

You have the option of building your own flight cage in case you do not want to invest in large cages that can be very expensive.

Building the enclosure on your own

There are various types of aviaries that you can build including outdoor aviaries or full wire aviaries. The designs and plans are easily available on the Internet. However, you need to have some basic considerations before you actually construct an enclosure for your bird.

You can get a wire enclosure constructed for as little as $10 and this is the most economical option available. This can be a super fun project. All you will have to do is dedicate a little time towards it.

The best type of aviaries to build are the free standing ones and not the permanent ones. That way it is also easy if you decide to move. Now, the only thing you need to remember with any permanent structure is that you may have to get permission from Zoning departments in your area.

Here are a few things you must consider before you construct an enclosure for your birds:

- Make sure you find a good location that is free from any traffic and noise.

- You should have access to water and safe electrical outlets.

- If the enclosure is indoors, you need to make sure that you give the birds ample air flow in order to be healthy.

- Indoor enclosures should be built in a way that they are easy to clean.

- You need to make sure that an outdoor aviary has good drainage. This will ensure that there are no damp floors which may lead to disease.

- In the case of the outdoor aviaries, it is also important to ensure that the area is safe from any pests or predators.

- As discussed before, the enclosure should be longer and not taller. You need to be able to provide ample floor space to each bird. A simple measure of 4sq.feet per pair should help you understand the size of the aviary.

- The cage door is the trickiest part of the enclosure. You need to make sure that it is easy to access while keeping the birds safe from any chance of escape.

After you have taken care of all these considerations, the next thing to do would be to make sure that you get the right material to construct the enclosure with. Here are a few tips to help you with that:

- You can get all the material that you require from any home development store.

- The material that you purchase should be safe and must be free from any toxins.

- It is best that you avoid the use of redwood, cedar and screen wood. Pressure treated wood should also be avoided.

- Any material that corrodes such as brass or copper should be avoided.

- Zinc and lead may lead to heavy metal poisoning. These elements are usually found in the paints used to construct the cage.

- If you must use galvanized hardware cloth, make sure that it is washed with vinegar fully.

- Furniture polish and metal polish must be avoided at all costs when you make the enclosure.

- It is a great idea to get PVC powder coated wiring because of the ease of maintenance.

- Plastic netting is only suitable for indoor cages as the outdoor ones will have rodents chewing into them in no time.

- Wiring should not have spacing more than ½" and less than ¼".

- Never use screens as the nails of the bird will get caught in it, leading to serious injuries.

The only other rule that you must keep in mind is to make the cage as large as you can afford. That way, your birds will have a lovely permanent home that they can live for the rest of their lives in.

How to position the enclosure

The most important thing with the enclosure is where you position it. You need to keep the safety and comfort of the bird in mind at all times. One thing with birds is that they tend to get really nervous if you tower over them all the time. The best way to position these cages is such that the perches are above your own eye level.

If you have placed the enclosure indoors, it is a good idea to have the enclosure near a window that can give the birds natural light. You also need to have a shaded area in the enclosure that the birds can rest in.

You need to make sure that the settings of the cage mimic natural light as closely as possible. If you need to provide artificial lighting, it is best that you provide full spectrum light. You need to set these lights to a timer that switches it on at dawn and switches it off at dusk, basically matching the sun rise and sun set. You will have to make seasonal adjustments to match the length of the day.

Lighting is the most important thing for your parakeets, as it plays an important role in the hormone cycle of the birds. This influences breeding.

You can opt for fixtures that emit UV lights, as UV light plays an important role in Vitamin D production and also calcium absorption in birds. You have to make sure that the cage is dark at night. Opting for a dim light is also a good idea to prevent any episodes of night fright.

There is no need to cover your cage at night. It is has been discouraged by a lot of bird lovers and owners as it can reduce the amount of fresh air that your bird gets. Also this may upset your bird's sleeping cycle as they may not wake up with the rising sun.

You need to give your bird a living area that is suitable for him. You need to keep the following points in mind to ensure that your home is bird proofed properly:

- Do not keep any cleaning agents near the cage as they may contain ammonia and Clorox fumes.

- The birds should be kept free from any chlorine fumes.

- Products that give out mists or fumes like air fresheners should not be placed near the cage.

- You should not have a combustion exhaust around the cage.

- Disinfectants containing pine oil should not be placed near the cage.

- Iron boards, heat lamps and pots containing Teflon should be kept away from the cage. When these surfaces are heated, they release a gas that is harmful for birds.

- Do not spray suede or leather protectant near the cage.

- Smoking near the cage area must be strictly prohibited.

- Be careful and watchful about gas leaks.

- Moth balls should never be placed near the cage.

- Scented candles may contain fumes that are poisonous for birds.

- Varnish and paint removers should be kept away from the bird.

- You also need to make sure that the cage door is closed well whenever you leave the room.

- If you plan to let the birds out of the cage for long periods, it is essential that you do not have any fans or table fans around the area.

The area that you choose to house your birds in should not have temperature fluctuations. The kitchen is one such example. You should also make sure that the area is not accessible to your other pets and is also free from any toxic plants. You can get the birds acclimatized to any temperature that is comfortable for you. All you need to make sure is that it does not fluctuate too much.

If your birds are going to stay outdoors, shade is absolutely necessary. If you live in an area where the temperature fluctuates, the cage should be placed in an area that is protected from this fluctuation. The plants that are around your aviary should be non-toxic and bird friendly.

It is absolutely mandatory to keep free ranging birds away as they may contaminate the food of your birds and also spread infectious diseases.

With these tips and ideas, you should be able to find the ideal space for your aviary. That way your birds are not only safe but are guaranteed to be happy in the area that they are going to spend the rest of their lives in.

Accessorizing the cage

Stimulating the bird and making sure that he gets ample exercise is one of your biggest responsibilities. The perches and accessories of the cage are essential not only for the physical exercise but are also important for feeding the birds and giving them ample visual barriers if you have multiple birds in your aviary.

The type of perch that you choose plays a very important role. If you opt for dowel perches, you may face issues like lack of foot exercise, as the bird may not get proper footing. These perches force the birds to shift all their weight on to one foot. As a result, in case there is an outbreak of bumblefoot, it may get aggravated.

Dowel perches may be included but should not be the only perch in your cage. Opt for perches that are made from nontoxic hardwood and clean material.

If you are planning to get a branch for your cage, make sure that it is obtained from a tree that has not been sprayed with any pesticides. Wood rot and mold should also be considered when you are bringing wood from the outdoors. The best option is to purchase manzanita branches that you will find in any pet store.

Although some people may tell you that sandpaper covered perches are good for your bird as it keeps the toe nail short, you must never opt for this. It leads to foot infections and bruises.

You must also place the perches such that they are not directly above one another or directly above the food and water bowls. This prevents any chances of contamination due to the droppings. Make sure that perches made of wood are replaced regularly as they become contaminated with time.

The next most important cage accessories are the food and water dishes. The only thing you need to remember is that these dishes should be very easy to clean. The best option for parakeets is a stainless steel cup. Metal containers having soldered ends should be strictly avoided as they may lead to lead poisoning.

The water and food bowls should be placed away from one another to encourage exercise. If you notice that your bird is nesting in the cups instead of feeding from them, you will have to shift to a tube style feeder.

You will not need too many toys for your parakeets. These birds are not so demanding in this department as compared to parrots. Adding a swing is a good idea as long as it does not get in the way of the bird's movements. It must also never strike the wall of the cage.

You may add other modes of entertainment in the cage including short strings tied to the roof of the cage. This string should not be made of small fibres and should not be too long as it may entangle the bird. About 2 inches is a good length for the strings.

Parakeets will also appreciate a place to roost in at night. A nest or a perch should do the trick. You can place it near the upper corners of the cage. If you make a roosting area with wood, avoid cedar and redwood or any other pressure treated wood. You can use shredded paper, coconut fibre or tissue paper. Remember that this roosting area will also encourage breeding among your birds.

The nesting or roosting area is not mandatory. However, if you have several birds in your aviary, getting sleeping tents for birds also gives them a good hiding area in case one or more of their cage mates become aggressive.

When it comes to accessories for parakeets, less is more. You have to make sure that the area is not too crowded. Flight should be comfortable as this the most preferred form of exercise as far as parakeets are concerned. This is also the most effective way of exercise for parakeets.

Keeping the cage clean

The bedding that you choose is an important part of hygiene. You need to make sure that whatever you choose is highly absorbent in nature. Some of the best options for parakeet cages include paper towels, computer paper, newspaper, paper bags, butchers' paper or just about anything that absorbs well.

Every night before you turn the lights out, you need to make sure that you take the substrate out and replace all the soiled layers.

The cages and perches should be cleaned out every week with mild liquid dish soap. You can scrub them well to make sure that any dry feces is removed entirely.

Disinfecting the cage once a month is essential. A weak solution of bleach that is about 1 gallon of water with ¾ cup of bleach should do the trick. This will get rid of all the organic substances including feces, food and feathers. You need to remove as much as you can manually before you apply this solution on to the cage.

Remove the birds from the cage when it is being cleaned. It is a good idea to have a small transfer cage that they can be housed in on a temporary basis. Bleach may be used only when the area is well ventilated. You should not use this solution on any metallic surface.

The cage should be dried fully before your birds are allowed into the cage. The birds must not come in contact with bleaching powder at any cost. You need to rinse the cage well and dry it in the sun before the birds are replaced.

Physical cleaning of the cage on a regular basis is one of the best ways to prevent diseases amongst your flock. One risk factor for the owners of birds is the inhalation of fecal dust and spores while cleaning the cage. This may aggravate respiratory problems.

The best thing to do would be to install an electrostatic type filter for the air. If your bird area has a central air system, you can prevent the transfer of pathogens.

Of course, all the food and water dishes must be cleaned every day. If you see any food in the bowls, you need to discard it and make sure that your birds get fresh food every single day. That will keep them healthy and will prevent the chances of any fungal or bacterial growth inside the enclosure.

2. Bird Proofing

A human home is seldom bird friendly. Our homes consist of glass items, Teflon coated pans and of course AC vents that seem normal and mundane to us. These simple household items can be hazardous to your bird and it is necessary for you to take the following measures to bird proof your home:

- Avoid using Teflon coated pans. These pans release certain fumes that can be fatal for a parakeet, or any other bird for that matter. If you cannot eliminate Teflon pans, you need to at least ensure that the housing area of the bird is away from the kitchen.

- Breakable items should be kept out of the flight path of your bird. It is best to avoid them altogether as they may cause serious accidents that you will most certainly regret. You can keep these delicate items in areas of the house that the bird will most likely not access.

- Lead weights on curtains and blinds should be removed as lead poisoning occurs quite easily when the bird comes in contact with it.

- Keep loose wires out of the way. Birds tend to tug at any loose wire and may get electrocuted in the process.

- Close the door to the kitchen. The kitchen has several hot items like pans, stove tops etc. that can cause serious burns to your bird if he sits on them unknowingly. If not, you can get special covers for these surfaces quite easily.

- Ceiling fans should be kept off whenever the bird is out of the cage. You must also avoid switching on table fans when the bird is flying around the house.

- Never keep plain glass windows spotlessly clean. Mark them by placing items like pots at the window sill. You can even add stickers to these clean glass surfaces to ensure that the birds do not fly right into them and suffer from injuries.

- The cage should be kept away from hard surfaces. If you have a baby bird, he may attempt to fly and fall several times in the process. A fall on a hard cement floor can be fatal to the bird.

- Keep the cage away from the air conditioner or the radiator. Cold or hot emissions from these machines can cause several health problems in parakeets. Keep the cage in an area of the house that is extremely cosy.

Once you have a bird in your home, you will always have to make sure that the doors and windows are shut. Whenever you put the bird back in the cage, lock the door properly. Also be careful when you open and close the door. If your bird is let out loose most of the time, slamming the door can lead to a trapped bird with multiple injuries. Lastly, be prepared to make changes as per the personality of your bird. All you need to remember is that any health risk should be out of the way entirely.

3. Introducing the bird to your Family

When you are bringing a parakeet home, it is natural for the family to be just as excited as you to welcome home a new member of the family. This bird is highly sensitive and will analyze every situation in your home before becoming a part of the household. So, you need to lay a few ground rules to prepare your family for the bird as well:

- The bird will not be disturbed during its initial days in your home. This includes no teasing, no bringing friends over to see the bird, no parties, no loud music and even no talking to the bird. That way, you can establish a sense of security with the new members.

- One must never stick their finger into the cage even for fun. These birds will bite when threatened. And, the bite will be powerful enough to rip a person's finger tip off.

- The responsibilities of feeding the bird will be divided. Initially, the other family members can be accompanied by the person whose bird it is. Then, they will have to do this on their own. Spending time feeding the bird, especially, helps the bird know all the members of the family and associate them with food, which is quite positive. Birds are not threatened by their family or their flock as long as they are part of the daily routine.

- Everybody will learn about the parakeet in complete detail. They can also attend the basic training classes with you if you are adopting your bird.

- No one will tease the bird with large and colorful objects like balls or toys. These things make the bird look at you like a predator and he will withdraw himself from you. They will also make the bird susceptible to behavioral issues if repeated persistently.

- Whoever leaves the house last will check all the doors and windows and will make sure that the cage is closed. If there are any other additional measures like separating the household pets, it should be done by this person. The person leaving the house last is responsible for taking all the safety measures with respect to the bird who will be left alone all day.

- Only one person in the house will take the responsibility of training the bird. If you use multiple methods or cues, the bird will simply get confused and will not respond to training effectively. This is usually done by the person who is closest to the bird or by someone who has better experience with training and caring for birds.

- Do not encourage the household pets to attack the cage even for fun. Cats or dogs are natural predators who may cause a lot of harm to your parakeet. In the case of this large bird, even vice versa is possible, considering the size and the power of this bird.

When you bring a parakeet home, you need to understand that you are bringing home a highly evolved life form. They understand the slightest changes in their ambience. It is the job of the entire family to ensure that they bird feels comfortable in the house and feels like a part of the flock.

Your family should be educated about the needs of parakeets to make sure that they are alert in case of any emergency. If nothing else, you need to make sure that they know how to provide first aid for common accidents like bleeding and broken feathers.

The whole family should be aware of where the first aid box is placed and where the supplies for the birds are located. They should also have the number of the vet on their phones. This way, you are all on the same page as far as first aid and emergency care is concerned.

The larger the flock, the happier a parakeet is. So make sure your family can be the ideal and most loving flock imaginable.

4. Parakeets and other pets

If the parakeets are your first pet, then all you really need to focus on is your new birds. However, if you are a parent to other pets as well, you have to make sure that you take care of the safety of your new birds as well as your existing pets.

Never take the personality of your pet for granted. Even the gentlest cat or dog can be very aggressive with pet birds. If you have birds as pets, too, you need to check if they are compatible with one another or not before you put them together.

You have to understand that these are animals with instincts. They all have a role to play in the ecosystem and will live up to it even if they are domesticated. If one animal is a prey animal and the other is a predator, the former will always overpower the latter. They will have that instinctive sense towards their prey and may attack when you least expect them to.

Parakeets, dogs and cats

Parakeets are really tiny birds which makes them a lot more vulnerable than a larger bird such as a cockatoo. When you are bringing a parakeet home to a house with pets like cats and dogs, you need to follow these safety guidelines to make sure that there are no accidents.

- Make sure that they are aware of each other's presence. Do not keep the birds away from the cats or the dogs all the time. When your bird is slightly accustomed to the new home, you can take the cage into the same room as the family cat or dog.

- If you have a cat or dog at home, the cage should be heavy and strong enough. Make sure that your cat or dog is not able to knock the cage over and get to the bird.

- When the cage is big, the bird is able to back up in case your pet is able to get his paws through.

- The cage should have several visual barriers in it. This includes roosting areas, large toys or even branches. That way the bird is able to hide in case he feels threatened. Even if your bird is not breeding, providing a nest box might be a good idea for his or her safety.

Even after taking all the possible precautions, you need to make sure that your bird and your pet are not left entirely unattended. There should be no interactions that are unsupervised, especially if your dog or cat isn't trained.

If you intend to leave your cat or dog alone with the pet, make proper introductions. When your pet stops showing signs of curiosity towards the cage of the bird, it means that he is accustomed to having him around. This is when you can let the bird out in your presence and see what happens.

You must have the dog or cat trained to "stay" or you must have the bird trained to "step up". Without this, you are only asking for a disaster.

Some owners are lucky that their pets and birds get along like two peas in a pod. Even if the bird does get out of the cage, it is not really a risk as the cat or dog may not even pay any attention. But, if you notice the slightest sign of aggression in your cat or dog towards the bird, do not attempt to leave them without any barrier.

This is when the cage becomes even more important. Now, even if your bird and pet are able to stay with one another without any physical stress, you need to stay on guard. This is because the size of birds, especially parakeets, is a lot smaller than your cat or dog.

While your pet may not intend to harm the bird, accidentally stepping or pouncing on the bird may be fatal. Bites of cats, especially, are toxic for birds. Needless to say, you can imagine the impact that a dog's bite would have on the body of the bird.

If you do have untoward accidents despite all the precautions, remember that it is not the fault of your pet. They act purely based on their instincts. While preparing your birds and pets for one another is a seemingly wonderful idea, it is certainly not fool proof.

Experts recommend that you keep your pets and birds separated with some sort of barrier. You may keep your dog or cat in an enclosure or you may want to get a good quality cage for your bird. The latter is always the better option. If you have an aggressive breed at home, make sure that you put both of them in enclosures when you leave the house for maximum safety.

Can you train your cat or dog to like the bird?
This is something that you may wish for as an owner. Of course, it is adorable to watch cats, dogs and birds play with one another. You can train your pet to understand what behavior is acceptable around the bird and what is not. But you can definitely not train them to lose their natural instincts. That is always the factor of doubt as far as pets are concerned.

Here are a few things that you may do if you are trying to train your cat or dog:

- Introduce the birds when they are younger. That is when the bird is more comfortable. If the bird is older, you will need to be able to handle the bird confidently before you start training the cat or dog. Just hold the bird up to the dog or cat and watch the reaction. If either one is uncomfortable, put the bird back and try again after a few days.

- If you notice your cat or dog trying to scare the bird or is putting the bird at risk with any action, you need to put an end to it instantly. A loud "NO" or "STOP" is good enough for your pet.

- You must never allow the cat or dog to climb over the cage or attempt to reach into it.

- It is easier to train your pet when they are younger. Kittens and puppies are usually not aggressive. But, their playfulness can be hazardous to your bird. If the pet pounces on your bird, it could lead to serious injuries and even death in extreme cases.

When you raise your pets all together, they are usually not aggressive. However, even the slightest provocation could be dangerous. For instance, if your bird is hormonal or brooding, he may become a lot more territorial than you expect.

This aggressive behavior during the breeding season is seen in females, especially if they have not been paired. In such cases, the attack may be initiated by the bird. If your dog or cat responds as a defense mechanism, it could still be fatal to the bird.

It is up to you to make sure that you understand any signs of behavioral changes in either animal. Unless pet owners are watchful and mindful of what their birds or cats are up to, interactions could be unpleasant.

That said, you also need to make sure that you train the bird to understand what behavior is acceptable and what behavior is not. The most important thing to do with parakeets is to ensure that they do not learn the habit of chewing. If they develop the urge to chew, they may even make the ear of the cat or dog their target and get into trouble. If you notice your bird reaching for the paw or the ear of your pet, put him back in the cage. This tells them that this behavior is not acceptable.

Whether you want to train your cat or dog to be around the birds or not is entirely a personal decision. Some owners never let their birds out of the cage in the presence of their other pets.

The only reason that training is recommended is to ensure that there are fewer chances of accidents if someone leaves the cage door open accidentally or if the bird flies out during the feeding or cleaning session. Training your pet makes them less interested in the bird over time and this is imperative in making accidents in the household less common.

Parakeets and other birds

Parakeets are timid birds, no doubt. However, not all varieties of parakeets are compatible with one another. Some of them can get really aggressive when kept in a mixed aviary.

With respect to parakeets, a mixed aviary refers to different types of parakeets and not different species of birds entirely. The rule of thumb with parakeets is that they are best when kept with birds that are of the same physical structure as them. This includes canaries and other parakeets. Large birds like parrots or cockatoos may not be the best option if you want to house the birds together.

Compatibility among parakeets is best understood when you study the nature of the birds in the wild. If they are social birds that are not restricted to pairs, then they will most likely get along well. However, if these birds get too territorial during the breeding season, you may want to study a little more about them before you keep them together.

It is best that you house your birds in pairs if you are going to keep them in a mixed aviary. You must at least ensure that there are equal numbers of male and female birds. That way the competition during the mating season will reduce, leading to less aggression.

If you already have an aviary or even a pet bird at home, the first thing you need to do is quarantine the new bird. You see, birds tend to be carriers of several diseases that can affect the whole flock. Even a seemingly healthy bird may develop health problems after the incubation period of these disease carrying microbes is completed.

The new bird must be kept in a separate cage in an entirely different room for at least 30 days. This is the incubation time of most of the parasites and microbes. If your bird shows any signs of illness within this period, you may return him to the pet store or the breeder if you have a valid health guarantee.

A health guarantee is normally provided for 90 days after the purchase of the bird. However, you need to make sure that the bird is checked by an avian vet within 72 hours of purchase.

The quarantining room should have a separate air source. This means you can keep the new bird indoors if the other aviary is an outdoor one. It is best that you keep the new bird in a different room altogether. Some even recommend asking a friendly neighbor to keep your new bird for a few days.

Make sure you handle the birds that are already in your home before you handle the new bird. This includes feeding, changing water containers etc. If you do handle the new birds first, take a shower and change your clothes and shoes before you handle the existing birds.

During this time you may want to treat your new bird for parasites such as coccidian, giardia etc. Stool samples not more than 42 hours old should do the trick.

After quarantining, you can bring the cage of the new bird into the same room as the other birds. If the other birds are larger birds, it is best that you do not house them in the same enclosure. If they are parakeets or sparrows, you will have to observe the birds well before you place them together.

Once you keep the cages in the same room, observe the reaction of the other birds. Do they become irritable and aggressive? If yes, you may consider keeping them in separate enclosures. However, if the other birds merely respond to the calls of the new bird, which will make them noisier than usual, it may not be such a bad idea to introduce your birds.

You can introduce the birds by putting them in a neutral enclosure. That way, neither bird is territorial or aggressive. Individual interactions starting with the least aggressive bird is the best option.

Once all the birds in your aviary have been introduced to one another, you can try to place your new parakeets in the mixed aviary too. Even the slightest sign of aggression means that you need to get your new bird out and house him separately.

There are a few things that will help you decide if certain birds will be compatible or not. First, you need to understand the habitat of the bird. Birds that are comfortable feeding off the floor of the aviary will usually be less aggressive. On the other hand, if the bird species has special requirements with respect to the feeding area, the nesting spot, etc., they are aggressive.

These birds tend to hijack the nesting areas of other birds leading to a lot of confrontations and aggression among one another. If you do have such birds in your aviary which includes the java sparrow, diamond fire tail parakeet, cut throat parakeet, red brown parakeet or the crimson parakeet, it is best that you do not mix your birds.

When you house mixed birds in one cage, you are creating a colony. So, always ask your vet or breeder if a certain species is a colony bird or not. Parakeets, for example, are successful colony birds. But, if you mix them with other species that aren't, you will be putting your birds at risk.

Even with successfully colonized birds, making sure that they get their individual space is mandatory. This means that each bird should have at least 2 cubic meters to himself. They also need to have their own perches and toys and also feeding containers that are easy to access and use. That way, you will have a peaceful colony of birds.

Chapter 4: Caring for Your Parakeet

Building a bond with your bird is constant work. From the first day of bringing your bird home, you have to make sure that he is on the way to becoming a happy and healthy member of your family.

The care that you provide for your bird has a big role to play in his health and in his ability to adjust to his new home. This chapter will tell you in detail about taking good care of your parakeet and ensuring that you have a pet who is happy and content.

1. Initial interactions

As excited as you may be to show off your new pet or even play with him the day he is home, it is best that you avoid it. For parakeets or any other bird, the first day in your home is their first day in a new environment. The bird is accustomed to the environment at the breeder's, the shelter or the pet store. Your house needs some getting used to. This can be made much easier if you let the bird settle down at his own pace and learn about his new home.

The first thing that you need to do is transfer the bird from the travel cage to the bird's actual cage. Open the door of the enclosure and place the door of the travel cage in front of it. Open the travel cage and wait for the bird to walk in voluntarily. That may take a couple of minutes. Be patient. Make sure you do not rush the bird and stress him out.

It is a really good idea to leave the bird alone with some food and water on the first day. They will not really like an unfamiliar voice. That said, it is a recommendation from many parakeet owners that you should spend time with the bird that you plan to buy while he is at the breeder's or the pet store. That makes the housebreaking process a lot easier.

If you have a bird that has been hand tamed, it is a lot easier to handle him eventually. However, on the first day even a hand tamed bird must not be meddled with. They need to recover from the traumatic experience of the drive and the whole shift to a new home.

When you are handling the food and the water bowls, make sure that you do not stand over the cage. You need to be at the eye level of the bird. That way, he will not look at you as a predator or as someone who is dominating him. You do not want to threaten your parakeet by towering over his cage. Once you have given him water and food, simply pretend like he does not exist and go about your routine. This is hard because you are obviously excited about having the new bird. However, avoid interaction on the first day.

A towel is really useful for a new bird. Put a towel on the back of the cage and let the bird hide behind it when he wants to. This is a popular technique that is used even for birds that have lived with a family for a long time. You see, our homes are filled with lights and sounds. It could be from the television, mobile phones and other appliances. They need at least 10 hours of sleep. This towel will help them hide from all the noise and just relax. You can even buy readymade curtains or tents that you can install for the birds to sleep in or behind.

Try not to talk to the bird as much as possible. You see, these creatures form very quick mental associations. Now, when the bird is stressed and you are constantly talking to him, he will relate your voice to stress. That will make the whole process of training him and bonding with him challenging for you. You may walk past the cage a couple of times to make him familiar with your presence. But, other than that, avoid any form of interaction on the first day.

The breeder or the pet store assistants should clip the flight feathers of your bird. Usually, this is already done. However, it is always a good idea to check. You do not want to come home and have your bird flying all over the house while transferring him to his enclosure. There are chances that you leave the cage door open accidentally. After all, you are not used to having a bird at home. Remember, if you have other pets at home, this is even more important to keep your bird safe.

For the first few weeks, you can progressively increase the interactions with your bird. To begin with, place your hands on the sides of the cage and see how the bird reacts. He will nibble at your fingers, come close to your hand and just try to feel you out a little bit. Let him get used to you.

The key is to make sure that your bird is in a place where he is able to see your family and your activities. That way, he familiarizes himself with your family. As people pass by the cage, the bird will take note of them and observe them very carefully.

Now, talking to the bird can be tricky. Make sure that you keep your voice as low as possible. Say the same phrase again and again. Use something common like, "Hello", "Hey baby", "Hi pretty bird" etc. This may also encourage your bird to mimic you. The reason you need to use the same phrase is that the bird does not really have a vocabulary yet. He will relate to the sounds that you make. The call must be familiar if you want the bird to relate to them and start responding to them.

You know that your bird is making progress if he walks towards the door of the cage when you arrive. That means that he is fond of you and is looking forward to the interaction with you. At all times, you need to bear in mind that you will only interact with the bird when you are at eye level. Let him feel like an equal to you. That is when he will start to get comfortable. It is best that these interactions are limited to one or two members of the family for the first few weeks.

Then, you may introduce the rest of your family to the bird, one by one. Let them start off with the hands on the sides of the cage as mentioned above. Parakeets will always bond with the whole family but will definitely pick favorites. These birds are really choosy whether it comes to the food, the toys or even the members of the family. If you take it slow, your bird will make some progress.

Then, when you think it is safe, just reach into the cage and offer your finger for a step up. If your bird is hand tamed, chances are that he will slowly perch on the finger. If not, you can follow the simple trust building tips that are mentioned in the following chapter.

Is your parakeet stressed?

For the first few days, the bird may not eat that well. This is not really an issue as long as you see that the bird is easing up and is progressing to better eating habits. However, in some cases, there may be something that you are doing unknowingly that is stressing the bird out very badly. You need to watch out for the following stress signs in your parakeet:

- Skin mutilation or tail plucking
- Sudden changes in personality from being extremely quiet to becoming unnaturally loud.
- Pacing up and down the cage. This may happen on the floor or on the perch.
- Pinning of the eyes.
- Keeping the tail feathers fanned at all times.
- Keeping the chest and head feathers raised all the time.
- Evident weight loss.
- Refusal to eat.
- Excessive urination.
- Too much water consumption.

If you see this behavior even up to the third day in your home, take the bird to an avian vet immediately. It may not just be stress but signs of some other health issue.

How to build trust?

Parakeets are highly intelligent creatures. You need to be aware of it at all times when you are interacting with your parakeets. It does not matter whether your parakeet is pleasant in his behavior or even aggressive, the first thing that you need to establish is that you are comfortable in the environment that he is in. That means, you need to keep him in a room where he can see you walking around and just being yourself.

After two to three days, your bird should be settled in quite comfortably. That is when you can introduce treats to your bird. The best treat to start out with is some type of seed. You can try feeding it with your fingers. But, if you see that he does not respond or is scared of your fingers, you can give it with a spoon or maybe on a stick. When the bird begins to relish the treat, he will take it from your fingers too. If he still doesn't take it from your hand, just take the seed with your fingers and place it next to the bird. Then when he comes for the treat, praise him. Continue just this for about a week. When he is eating out of your hands comfortably, the next step is to let him out of the enclosure. It may take up to two weeks at the most to reach this stage.

Make sure that the wings of your birds are clipped before you let him out of the cage. If that is not what you want to do, you must establish a secure environment for the bird before you let him out. This is a checklist that you need to follow before you let out a bird without clipped wings at ANY time:

- All the windows must be closed with the screens pulled down
- There should be no hot stove tops
- Close the lids of the toilets
- Keep all the doors shut
- There should be no new people the first time
- You should definitely not have other pets around until they have had a chance to bond
- The fans should all be off

Allow him to explore the area around the cage. He may perch on the door or maybe on the cage itself. When he is settled somewhere comfortable, give him a treat. What you need to know about parakeets is that they may not really leave the cage and go too far as they are inherently territorial. And when you put a treat into the food bowl, they will go back into the enclosure easily. If he does fly far, you can still lure him with a trail of his favorite treat. This is the initial stage of building trust that you need to work on before you get him to perch on your finger or on your shoulder.

2. What to feed Parakeets?

Many first time owners are quite confused about what to feed their birds. There is a lot of contrasting information about what is good for your bird and what isn't. So it can be a little hard. That said, there are few things that are worth knowing about parakeets:

- They are not fussy eaters but they pick their favorites.
- Overfeeding can make them gain weight.
- They need a lot of vitamins and calcium.
- The food consumed may increase during the breeding or mating season.

Getting the basics right

Parakeets eat a large variety of foods including seeds, nuts and fresh fruits and vegetables. Some parakeet owners also give their pets eggs in small portions. If your parakeet develops a liking for this, you can even leave a small amount of the shell on, as it is very good for the birds.

To begin with you need to find a certain measure of the food that you are giving your parakeet. It can take a while to get the exact amount in place and you may even have to do a few trial and errors to see how much your parakeet will eat in one sitting. But, it is a good idea to go by tablespoon measures.

The truth about pellets

The first thing that you need to give your parakeet is dry pellets. Choose natural pellets from brands like Zupreem or Harrisons. If you choose the former, it can make up for 30% of your bird's diet but if you choose the latter, it should not be more than 10% of your bird's diet. The rest of it should contain fruits and veggies along with treats.

Avoid colored or dyed pellets as they may harm the bird. Pellets are made from crushed seeds and are full of fiber. They include a lot of vitamins and minerals such as calcium along with fruits and vegetables. These are all essentials in your parakeet's diet. You can start the day out with these pellets and actually make them the base of the diet. You can give a parakeet about 2 tablespoons of dry pellets in a day.

Pellets are best stored frozen. Brands like Zupreem may spoil easily and need to be frozen. Pellets contain several nutrients and are hence a lot better for your bird than an all seed diet. Only seeds can cause health issues in the bird. Give your parakeet fresh pellets every morning. Remove the left overs and refill the food bowl every day.

Adding seed treats in between the pellets is a great idea and necessary for your bird's diet. You get seed treats like nutriberries that will add a lot of minerals and vitamins to the Parakeet's diet. Ideally birds as small as the parakeet will consume about 2 to 4 of these in the day. You can give them in between meals, ideally when they are half done with the pellets and once the pellets are fully done. There are other such treats as well that birds may like and you should be able to find them in any store.

Fruits and Vegetables

These are crucial parts of a bird's diet. Although some avian vets will tell you otherwise, many parakeet owners will tell you from their personal experience that these birds need fruits and vegetables in order to stay as healthy as possible. Even in the wild, birds eat fruits and vegetables. So that is great for them.

You should ideally give a parakeet 1 tablespoon of vegetables and 1 tablespoon of fruits in a day. If you think that they will eat more, you must increase the vegetable portion. Vegetables give the birds a larger amount of Vitamin A that is essential for them. Fruits also give them the vitamins that they need but also act as flavor addition to the bird's food.

In order to offer the fruits or vegetables, you can mix two or more varieties of each and heat them a little bit in the microwave, just to make them warm. Then, you may mash them and feed them to your bird. Now, sometimes birds may not develop any taste for these fruits and vegetables so you can add stronger flavors like strawberry or blueberry juice. These are great foods to include but always remember that the portion of vegetables must be higher than fruits. Here are some good fruits and vegetable options for your birds:

Grapes
Apples
Pomegranate
Melon
Mango
Pineapple
Papaya
Kiwi
Watermelon
Star fruit
Blueberries
Cherries
Blackberries

Broccoli
Carrots
Beans
Sweetcorn
Peppers
Spinach
Sweet potato
Butternut Squash
Red Cabbage
Beetroot
Sprouts

You can divide the 1 tablespoon portion across the day and feed them to your bird. You must offer this separately from the pellets and you will notice that you bird will pick his favorites. Offering seasonal fruits and vegetables can be great for your bird. But, before you introduce any new food to the parakeet, ask a vet or do enough research to be sure that it is safe.

Important nutrients for parakeets

Some nutrients are more important than others for your parakeets. Here are a few nutrients that you need to make sure are part of your bird's diet.

Calcium

Calcium is one of the most important minerals for your bird. Sometimes, your avian vet may recommend some supplements. Until such time try to find natural sources of calcium for your bird. Pellets are the best option for a steady calcium source as most of them are fortified. You also get calcium perches and toys that the bird can enjoy and get his nutrients from.

Now just like us humans, birds need Vitamin D in order to synthesize the calcium. All parakeets need full spectrum sunlight. So you need to take them out at least once a day for good sunlight. You can take the cage out if possible. If not, you get special transparent cages without filters that are safer and easier to use. If possible, place the cage near a good enough source of sunlight for everyday access. It shouldn't be too bright or hot, however.

What not to feed your birds

- **Peanuts:** While other nuts like hazel nuts can be great for the parakeet, as they are a source of high protein, peanuts can cause health problems because of fungal toxins.

- **Onions and Garlic:** These two should not be offered in any form to the parakeets as they cause some irritation to begin with. In addition to that, they can make your parakeet very anemic.

- **Tomatoes:** Tomatoes, especially raw ones, are hazardous to birds as they are acidic vegetables. They potentially cause ulcers in parakeets.

- **Mushrooms:** They can cause serious digestive issues and even liver failure in parakeets.

- **Celery:** If you can remove all the stringy part of celery, it is quite safe to feed to your parakeet. If not, it may lead to crop impactation.

- **Avocados:** Avocados are poisonous for parakeets in general. They contain a certain toxin called perrsin that can cause breathing difficulties or even kill your parakeet in worst cases.

When you are uncertain of a certain food, be sure that you consult your vet or fellow parakeet owners. When you are sure that it is of no harm to your bird, you can introduce the birds to it.

What if the bird dislikes pellets?

This is a common problem faced by parakeet owners. Usually our birds come home from a pet store or from breeders. If they have been accustomed to a seed diet here, they may not take an instant liking towards pellets. Most parakeets who are on a mainly seed diet will experience some health issues or the other, the most pressing one being obesity.

One great way to introduce your bird to pellets is to include a small amount in the current seed diet. Then when he begins to eat that small amount, you may increase it. Keep increasing the proportion of the pellets till the seeds are completely out of the diet.

Another way to go about this is to give your parakeet mashed pellets. You can soak pellets in warm water until they are soft enough to crush. You can offer this to the bird and see if he or she eats it. If not, you can add a small amount of a flavor inducer such as agave syrup, cranberry juice or even sunflower kernels to the crushed pellets. Make sure that you just add a tiny pinch of flavor that is enough to attract the bird but not so much that it makes your parakeet addicted to that flavor.

Whenever you are making a change in your parakeet's diet, consult your vet. It is important to make sure that this diet change is not causing weight loss in your bird. You can monitor this at home on a scale or you have to work alongside an avian vet.

Sunflower seeds can be beneficial to your bird in very small amounts, maybe once a week. They do cause rapid weight gain but when given sparingly can be a great source of protein and Vitamin E.

The feeding routine

The final question is how often should you feed your parakeet? Ideally feeding the bird twice with a few treats in between can work really well. So in the morning offer the pellets first. Then at about 11am, you can give the bird one serving of vegetables. Then in the evening at about 4pm, you can give him the portion of fruits. Now in between these meals you may offer seed treats like nurtiberries. Establish a routine with your parakeet to ensure that he is eating on time.

Also measure the amount of food per meal to make sure that your bird does not overeat. You will know that your bird is done eating at a given meal time when he shows loss of interest in the food. Offer him only this much per sitting to avoid overeating. Only the pellets can be made available all day. That should also be done in controlled proportions of 2 tablespoons a day. Replace the water in the dish regularly as parakeets may dip their food in water and mess it up.

3. Keeping the cage clean

It is mandatory that you have a daily cleaning routine for the main parts of the cage. If you are not willing to do this, you must not commit to having a parakeet. Here are some simple practices that will make sure that your bird has a healthy and sanitary environment.

The right cleaning material

The cleaning material that you choose should be safe for the bird and must be able to thoroughly disinfect the cage of the bird. A bird's cage is full of pathogens that you need to clean up fully.

You may use soap and water if there is any organic material or debris that you want to remove. The solution must be very mild to prevent any irritation. Remember that soap and water does not disinfect the cage. You need to wipe the cage down with a disinfectant to make sure that it is actually free from germs and microbes.

Bleaching powder is one of the best and most easily available disinfectants. You can make a dilute solution and wipe all the contents of the cage down. Make sure that your bird is out of the cage when you do this. The fumes can irritate the bird. You can put him back after the solution has dried completely and the distinct smell is gone. If the cage is made of metal, bleaching powder may reduce its life.

An alternative is Nolvasan which is readily available in any pet store. You could also use Virosan as it is safer for your bird. Although these products are expensive, they are very useful for the cleanliness of your bird's cage. Most of the pathogens will be eliminated with these products.

Stabilized chlorine dioxide is also a good choice to disinfect the cage. The advantage with this product is that it uses oxidation to disinfect. That makes it effective even against spores and viruses. This product is also very safe. It is used to clean drinking water in many parts of Europe. There are no side effects or damages caused by the use of this product. It is also safe to clean the feeders and the water bowls with this product as it is completely safe. You just have to spray it on the surface that you want to clean and wipe it down. And, voila! Your bird's cage is free from any threats.

The cleaning schedule

There are some things that you have to do on a daily basis to ensure overall cleanliness of the cage. You can clean the cage thoroughly on a weekly or fortnightly basis. Here is a schedule that you can maintain for cage cleaning.

Daily cleaning

The food and water containers must be cleaned on a daily basis. If you use steel or porcelain ones, they are easiest to clean. It is a good idea to keep a spare pair that you can use when the ones that you have washed are drying. Use a cleansing gel that you can get in a pet store to clean the bowl. Then, rinse it with water thoroughly. Never leave any chemicals behind as it may seriously harm your bird. These bowls need to be fully dry before they are replaced.

The substrate needs to be removed and replaced on a daily basis. Most of the moisture is retained in the substrate and should be removed to prevent any fungal or bacterial growth.

Any surface that is exposed must be wiped down on a daily basis. You can use one of the disinfectants mentioned above in a very dilute form, spray it on the surface and then wipe it down after leaving it on for about 100 minutes. This is one way to make sure that your cage is sanitized and clean. In addition to that, it also increases the life of the cage.

Weekly or fortnightly cleaning

It is a good idea to remove all the toys from the cage every fortnight and clean them thoroughly. Any severely damaged ones can be thrown away. Use a brush to remove any dry organic matter. If you notice that one of the toys is very dirty, wash it immediately and dry it before replacing it. Soak the toys in a cleansing solution and rinse them completely. No chemical from the cleaning agent should be left behind, as it is harmful for your bird. Then, make sure that they are fully dry before you put them back in the cage.

Make it a monthly practice to wash the cage out thoroughly. You will have to use a brush to scrub out any dry material from the floor or the cage. Using warm water makes it easier to clean the dirty parts of the cage very easily. You can simply use a soap water solution.

Then, wash and rinse the cage fully. Once it is dry, spray a disinfectant and wash it down. Of course, you will have to have a stand by enclosure for your bird. Do not put the bird back until the cage is fully dry.

Some of you may want to keep the cage outdoors. Then, you must wash the whole cage twice a month. That will make sure that any pathogens that have been released into the cage by wild birds or rodents will be removed. It will also keep dust at bay.

If your bird has not been hand trained, you will need to use a towel to handle the bird. Wrap the towel around his body. Allow the ends to fall over your hands and protect them from any bites. Make sure that the head is not covered by the cloth. You can also use sturdy gloves to protect yourself from accidents.

The cage that you transfer your bird into must have a lot of food and water if this is the first time. Once the bird is trained and accustomed to this routine, it will be a lot easier for you. In case you are unsure of what cleansing agent you can use, consult your vet first. It is recommended that you check the cage thoroughly every day. In case you find any debris or peculiar droppings, clean it instantly. You definitely do not want to leave pieces of rotting food around. With all species of parakeets, you will also have to clean out the things that they hoard in their cage as part of their nesting habits.

4. Grooming your Parakeet

Grooming is not just important to keep the bird clean. It is also a very important part of bonding with your bird. In the wild, parakeets groom one another to show affection. You can maintain a regular grooming routine with your bird, too.

This will also help you discover any abnormalities on the bird's body or in the plumage. This could be a sign of underlying health issues. Grooming helps you detect them early so that your bird can get immediate medical attention.

Bathing your parakeet

In general, parakeets like to stay clean. They have several instinctive cleaning methods in the wild. You need to be able to provide the one factor that the birds miss, which is rain, through a regular bath. Now, as you know, parakeets are from tropical parts of the world where rainfall is common. So, that is essential for them to stay clean. Besides that, they have natural way of keeping their bodies free from any dirt.

How they clean themselves

Powdering down: This refers to a small amount of dander or powder that the birds produce from the feathers. All parakeets have certain down feathers that continue to grow for long periods of time. These feathers have very fine extensions that break often. This powder coats the feathers and the body of the bird. This powder repels water and dirt. It sticks to the dirt and when the bird preens itself, falls down with the dirt. The more dander the bird produces, the healthier he will be. Of course this is not a welcome instinct for most pet parakeets.

Preening: This is the healthiest natural grooming method for the birds. It is useful to scape feathers and keep them moist. You will see your parakeet use the water from the bowls to preen himself. Besides that, preening ensures that all the feathers of the bird are in place and can be used properly. In the wild, parakeets of any kind will not let one feather go out of place because it makes them more vulnerable to predator attacks. A feather sticking out means that the predator will be able to spot the bird in a flock.

When they preen themselves, these birds also break a certain gland known as the preen gland, or the uropygial gland, that is present just at the base of the tail. This gland produces a certain oil that the birds rub all over their feathers just to make them water proof.

How to bathe your parakeet?

If this is the first time your parakeet is taking a bath in your home, you need to make it a pleasant memory for him. Sometimes, when they have been bathed very harshly in their younger days at the breeders' or at the pet store they will develop a negative feeling towards bathing. They may scream and rant when they hear the sound of a water tub filling up.

In order to give your parakeet a bath, just fill up a small bird bath or even sink with water and lead the bird to it. You can use toys or treats to do this. Allow them to stand at the edge of the sink and just explore. They may be excited but scared to get into the water.

In order to lower the parakeet into the tub, allow them to perch on your palm and slowly lower him towards the water. Then let the bird step in. In about ten seconds of entering the water tub, the bird should become familiar with or just used to it. Keep talking to your bird and make him feel safe. Praise him when he is wading in the water. You can also put some of his favorite toys into the water.

If you need to use soap, it is safe to use any mild human soap or shampoo. But, it is recommended that you buy specially made soaps to avoid any sort of allergy or infection. You can make a diluted soap solution and use your hands to give him a lather. Take a lot of care to avoid getting any into his eyes. In case of thick dirt, you can use a wash cloth or a very soft tooth brush to gently brush it off. Then rinse the bird well with clean warm water and use a towel to pat him dry.

Some parakeet owners use hair dryers to dry their birds. But it is recommended that you let the bird dry naturally as this gives them a chance to even preen their feathers into place. Of course, you need to make sure that the air-conditioning and the fans are off in the room where the bird is drying himself off.

For fully grown parakeets, a bath is not necessary. You can simply spray some water on them or just allow them to walk around under the shower. You will get special shower perches in any pet store that allow you to place the perch on the tiles of the shower wall with suction cups. Avoid using soaps during showers as your bird may not allow you to get it all off. They will only stay under the shower for a few minutes and fly off. This is just to make up for their instinctive love of the rain.

You can give your bird a thorough bath every fortnight. A light shower is recommended twice in a week to keep the bird healthy and free from any infections. When you are putting them in a bird bath, make sure that it is very shallow as parakeets are not good swimmers as a general rule. It should just be enough for the bird to soak himself.

Nail and beak trimming

This grooming process is optional. If you notice that your bird's toes and beak are getting stuck in the toys or any fabric, you can trim them to avoid any accidents. If the beak or toe of your bird is stuck to the fabric on your upholstery and he tries to move suddenly, there are chances that the whole toe is ripped off or the beak is severely damaged. To avoid this, trim the sharp ends.

Wrap the bird with a towel, only exposing the part that you want to trim. In the case of the beak, gently lift the upper mandible with your finger and feel the sharp end. Keep the beak supported and trim the beak using a nail file. When you feel that it is just blunt, stop trimming. If the nail or the toe is too short, the bird will be unable to climb and hold properly.

Even with the toe, make sure that you have a finger supporting the nail you want to trim to avoid any chances of breakage or unwanted damage.

It is a good idea to give your bird perches and toys of different textures. That will let the nails and the beak stay blunt naturally. As the bird climbs or chews with the proper toys, the beak and nails get trimmed. You will see them rubbing their beak onto rough surfaces as an attempt to keep them trimmed. This is an instinctive practice that should be encouraged.

Remember that bonding with birds as intelligent as parakeets requires a lot of effort from your end. These birds will analyze every situation that they are put into and even the slightest doubt will break their trust. If you have adopted a bird that has been abused, this will take a longer time. You will also need a lot of assistance from your avian vet to gain the trust of such birds. Take it one step at a time and make sure that you do not rush him.

Wing clipping

Some people believe that wing clipping is not ethically correct. If you are one of them, make sure that your home is a safe haven for your bird. You do not want to have any flight related accidents at home. This may also lead to escape and loss of your precious parakeet.

If you have pets at home, do not clip the wings. This is your bird's only form of defense. Even when you have multiple birds in an aviary, the wings should be intact to help your bird escape an aggressive cage mate.

If you decide to clip your bird's wings, make sure you have it done at the vet's the first time. You can learn how to do it, practice with your vet and then do it at home. You need to be very experienced to ensure that you do not accidentally get any blood feathers.

A bird must be hand tamed before you decide to clip his wings yourself. He must be comfortable enough to let you handle him. The first thing is to get your bird into a comfortable position to clip his wings. Pick him up using a towel and place him face down on your thigh. Then let the first wing out of the loose end of the towel and spread the feathers. Cut the primary feathers only. These are the largest feathers. The first three feathers are usually cut. You can snip about 1cm from each feather.

Then, repeat on the other side. Compare the wings to make sure that they are equal. If they are not, your bird will have difficulty walking or even perching. In case you do get a blood feather, make sure you apply styptic power to the wound immediately. If the bleeding does not stop, take the pet to the vet to have the shaft removed.

Clipping the wings only reduces your bird's ability to fly. It does not prevent flight altogether. So, when you take your bird outdoors, be vigilant. Even the slightest breeze can give him the lift he needs and lead to an escape. You need to clip the wings every 6 months. With these playful birds, trimming of toe nails or beaks is not always necessary, as they will do it themselves by scraping the sharp surfaces off on any rough object like the wooden perch.

5. Understanding the language of your bird
Birds do communicate with us. It is up to the owners to spend time understanding the bird and learning the language of the birds. Birds use two methods to communicate- vocalization and body language. This is quite consistent and with regular interaction with your bird, you will be able to understand what your bird is trying to communicate with you.

Understanding vocalization or sounds

Parakeets can be extremely vocal birds. In fact, they have the reputation of being too noisy and talkative. This is quite a good thing, however, because your bird will constantly communicate with you. There are some noises and sounds that your bird will make. Becoming familiar with this will help you understand what to expect.

- **Talking, whistling and singing:** This means that your bird is happy and content.

- **Chattering:** The most commonly used method to get your attention. This is seen in birds that are still learning to talk.

- **Clicking the tongue:** They are just having fun or are asking you to do something fun with them.

- **Low growl:** This is a sign of aggression and shows that something is troubling or threatening the parakeet. Look for objects that your bird dislikes and get it out of their sight. Never handle a growling parakeet.

Understanding the body language of parakeets

Most of the communication takes place through the body language of the bird. Watching the way the bird stands, moves, uses his wings or his beak will tell you a lot about what he is thinking and feeling. Here are some typical parakeet gestures and postures that you should keep an eye out for.

- **Flashing the pupils**: All parakeets can control their pupils. If they dilate it, it is an indication of pleasure, anger or nervousness. You need to examine the surroundings of the bird to understand what this "pinning" or "flashing" signifies.

- **Tongue clicking**: This is a sign of pleasure and is often an invitation to you to come and play with him.

- **Beak clicking**: A sharp clicking sound made from the beak shows that your bird is feeling threatened. There could be some object or person in the room that the bird is scared of. He will additionally raise a foot and also extend his neck almost as if he is defending the cage.

- **Beak grinding:** You will hear the bird grinding his beak mostly at night. This is a sign of satisfaction and security.

- **Beak wiping**: When the bird is in an aviary, this is a sign of defense against the other birds or a warning sign. If your bird is alone and displaying this behavior, he is trying to get something out of his beak.

- **Regurgitation**: This behavior is displayed before their mates. Usually, a bird will regurgitate food and feed the contents to its partner. This is just what he is trying to do if he has a strong bond with you.

- **Head shaking**: If your bird moves the head from side to side almost like he is dancing or waving the head, he is trying to get your attention. The bird will even tilt his head to one side and look at you as a sign of interest towards what you are doing.

- **Lowering the head**: The bird will pull his wings close and lower the head and will almost look like he is about to fly. This is his way of telling you that he wants to come to you.

- **Beak fencing:** This is only seen when there are multiple birds in the cage. The birds will hold each other's beak almost like they are jousting. It is considered to be some sort of sexual behavior.

- **Panting:** If your bird is overheated or is too exhausted, then panting is observed. It is basically a sign of discomfort.

- **Wing drooping:** This is normal in young birds. If your bird is an adult, then it is a sign of illness.

- **Wing flipping:** A sharp flip or flick of the wing shows displeasure. It could also mean that your bird is just trying to set his feathers in place.

- **Quivering:** If the body or wings quiver, it is a sign of distrust. Talk to such a bird in a calm and comforting voice.

- **Marching:** if the bird marches with his head down, he is being defensive or aggressive. On the other hand if his head is up, he is inviting you to play with him.

- **Tail bobbing:** This is usually a sign of sickness or fatigue, especially when the tail bobs when your bird is breathing.

- **Tail wagging:** When the bird sees his favorite person or toy, he wags his tail as a sign of happiness.

- **Tail fanning:** This is a dominant or aggressive behavior that basically tells you to back off.

- **Barking:** The bird is not mimicking another pet in your home. This is a natural vocalization that that is meant to show dominance.

- **Purring:** If the bird's body is relaxed when he is purring, it shows contentment. However, if the body is still and the pupils are dilated, it is a sign of aggression.

- **Chattering:** You will hear the bird chattering or mumbling. He is only making his presence felt and is trying to get your attention.

Learning these simple postures and vocalizations of the birds can help train the birds better, too. You will also enjoy playing with your bird a lot more when you are familiar with his language. It is a great insight into the personality of your bird.

6. Cost of Owning a Parakeet

Now that you are aware of all the care that your parakeet needs, let us take a look at the monetary responsibility that you will be taking on by bringing a parakeet home.

- Cost of the parakeet: $200-400 or £100-250 depending upon the age, the breeding conditions and the source that you but them from.

- Cage: $150-400 or £80-200 depending upon the features available and the size. This is a one- time investment and it is recommended that you get the best.

- Food: $40 or £25 every month.

- Toys: This really depends upon the type of toys that you buy. But you will shell out a minimum of $15 or £10 on each toy that you buy.

- Wing clipping: If you get your bird's wing clipped by a professional, then you will spend about $15 to £10 every four months.

- Veterinarian Cost: You will spend at least $50 or £30 per visit to your veterinarian. You can expect annual costs of about $1200 or £650 per year.

- Pet Insurance: Depending on the kinds of cover that you are getting, your pet insurance may cost anything between $150-280 or £80-150 every month.

Make sure your budget is in place before you bring the parakeet home. Also be very sure that you can afford to take care of the bird as the costs will be ongoing for 20-30 years.

Chapter 5: Training your Parakeet

Parakeets are extremely intelligent birds. Training them is a major part of bonding with them. You can teach them simple and advanced tricks quite easily. Training is also a great mental activity for your bird.

With a bird like the parakeet, mental stimulation is extremely important in keeping the bird healthy and free from any bad behavior. A bored parakeet can be a nightmare as they develop issues like feather plucking or screaming.

1. Basic training

Basic training includes a few commands that your bird should be able to understand. These commands are extremely necessary when your bird is let out of the cage. They ensure that your bird is safe and that you are able to handle your bird easily when he is outside.

Step up training

Step up training is the best display of trust towards the owner. Now, not only does the step up training form the basis of building the relationship, it is also one of the most important things to teach your parakeet. In case of any emergency such as a fire or a natural disaster, you should be able to reach in and have the bird step up on your finger in order to escape. If you do not train the bird to step up, he may not let you handle him and pet him either. That makes it very difficult to do the other fun things like teaching him tricks and generally including him in various activities throughout your day.

Here are a few tips to train your bird to step up:

- Your hands are very scary for a new parakeet. Also, their cage is their home. When you just intrude and put your hands through, you are most likely to get bitten. So take it as slow as you possibly can.

- You will need a lot of treats that you can feed them with your hands if they are comfortable or with a spoon or a stick. When you have successfully taught your parakeet to come out of the cage, you are ready to have them step up on your finger.

- The first thing to do would be to lead the bird to the open door of the cage. Then, you can offer your finger like a perch just a few centimeters away from the door.

- Remember to hold the finger horizontally so that it looks like a branch and do not point at the bird in such a way that your fingers look like food to them.

- Then, hold the treat behind the perch finger.

- At this point, they may immediately step up or may hesitate. Do not stress them too much.

- Offer the step up command about two to three times and if the bird only looks at the treat and does not come for it, put the treat back in the food bowl and try again.

- It is also possible that your bird will put his beak around your perch finger and gently nibble. They are not biting and you must never draw your hand back. In the wild, birds do this to make sure that the perch is steady. So, if your bird bites your finger and you hold it still, he will probably step up. But if you draw the finger away, he will lose trust in your finger.

- When he climbs up, offer him a treat. Let him stay for a while and put him back in the cage.

- Offer him a final treat before closing the cage door.

- Keep doing this for a few days. Place your perch finger, say "Step Up" and when he does, offer a treat. Soon, just the step up command without the treat is good enough. Remember to praise your bird abundantly irrespective of whether he makes progress or not.

- After you have taught the bird to step up on your finger, you can offer your shoulder as the next step.

- You will do the same thing, hold the bird up to your shoulder and when he steps on to it, offer him a treat. That way you can lead him up to your head as well.

- Getting the bird on your shoulder is great progress as it allows you to include him in all your daily activities. You can keep him on your shoulder as you fold laundry, do the dishes or even just sit down and read a book. That way, he will feel like you are giving him attention and is likely to bond faster.

Once you have established the trust to get the parakeet to step up on to your finger, you can try to pet him. Start by stroking the head and the cheeks. If he allows you to do that, you can move on to the critical part which is touching the beak. If your parakeet allows you to touch the beak without biting, then it means that he has established a high level of trust in you.

Teaching your parakeet not to bite

There are two reasons why your parakeet may bite- defense and attention. However, biting of any kind must be discouraged. The bird must know that it is not acceptable behavior. Also, if you are able to build trust with the parakeet, biting will significantly stop. There are other things that you can try to stop your bird from biting.

In the initial days of your interaction with your parakeet, biting only comes from fear. So, you need to be patient. If your bird bites you when you are trying to get them to perch on your finger, you have to remember not to shout or scream.

The moment you do that, the bird gets a message that this is how they can control you and stop you from doing what they are not fond of. Instead, you just let the bird back in the cage and try again.

The next thing is when your parakeet has started perching on your hand but begins to bite when you are trying to pet it. That is when you have a little more trust with the bird.

Then, you can gently push the head down with your index finger. It is a small and slight push that should not hurt the bird. Then in a very soft voice say "No biting". Then attempt to pet the parakeet again till you have a positive reaction.

Just stroking the cheek is good. When this happens, praise the bird for being good, put the bird back in the cage and give him a closing treat. At this stage, the bird finds the cage to be a positive reinforcement.

The last type of biting that you want to discourage is "demand" bites. This is when you have established a good relationship with your bird and he nips at you when he wants something that is in your hand. For instance, if he is on your shoulder and you have a fruit in your hand, he will bit your ear or cheek. There are two things that you can do.

First, you can just return the bird to the cage. This stops the behavior as the bird wants to be with you at this stage and going back to the cage is not as much fun as being with you.

The next thing is to shake his balance. If he is on your head or shoulder, you can actually run or jog. That puts the bird off balance and will make him release the beak. If he is on your finger, you can gently shake your hand or simply raise your elbow. This will put him off balance and make him release the beak. Now losing balance is something that parakeets hate and will give up any behavior that leads to it.

Stopping your parakeet from screaming

As mentioned before, parakeets can be extremely noisy. They can even begin to scream to seek attention or to make you do something they want you to. Both of these are not good and must be curbed.

Now, there are certain times of the day when the bird calls out instinctively. This is usually at dawn or dusk. Although this can be loud and extremely noisy, it is instinctive behavior. You must be sure that you can deal with some noise during the day. Also, make sure your neighbors do not complain.

The only time the screaming becomes a problem is when your parakeet begins to scream every time you leave the room. That means he is only screaming for your attention and nothing more. So, here are a couple of things that you do not want to do when you observe this behavior:

- Do not scream back at the bird and say, "Stop" or "Don't Scream".

- Do not come running back into the room every time to just get him to stop screaming.

- This encourages screaming. When you respond with your own voice or by coming to the bird, you are doing exactly what they want. You are their "Flock" that is calling back when they call. So they are happy to have your attention and will continue to scream.

- Unlike dogs or cats, a sharp "No!" is actually not a negative thing for birds. They think of it as your call in response to theirs.

- Instead, it is a good idea to put some toys or treats in the cage before you leave the room. That way they have something more interesting and something to distract them. It tells them that you going away means that it is time for some fun inside the cage.

- The next thing you can do is just let the bird scream and not come back. Wait for the screaming to stop and then go in and reward your bird. That way the bird understands that you will come back when he is quiet and will also reward him. Eventually, the period of silence will increase.

- Some people will tell you to put a blanket on the cage when the bird screams. While this works, it is negative reinforcement. Hence, it is discouraged.

2. Advanced training
Do not move on to these commands and tricks unless your bird has mastered the ones mentioned above. This can be extremely

confusing for the bird and can make the task a lot harder on your part.

Potty training

Surprisingly, it is possible for you to potty train a parakeet. It just requires you to understand the pooping cycle and body language of your bird.

A small bird like the parakeet will poop every 10 to 15 minutes and if you want to avoid accidents when your bird is out of the cage, you need to potty train him. Here are some simple tricks to teach your bird to poop where you want them to.

- The first thing to do would be to teach him to poop inside the cage in the morning.

- Before feeding, put a paper on the floor of the cage and wait for the bird to poop.

- They will show a very distinct type of body language which is usually lifting their tail and leaning down on the perch. Then, when they do poop, praise them abundantly and offer a treat which is part of the diet.

- The next step is to watch for these signs after you have taught your bird to step up.

- When you see the pooping body language, hold them over a trash can or over a piece of paper. Then when they do poop on that, they need to be praised abundantly.

- That way, they know that there is one place or appropriate place for them to poop and they will not mess the whole house up.

Teaching your bird to talk

Birds merely mimic what we say. So repeating words and phrases before the bird is the best way to train them to talk. If you say hello every time you see the bird or "food time" every time you feed him, he will pick up on it and will say the word before you do some days. When he does, give him loads of treats and praise him abundantly.

Speaking to the bird every day and saying the words that you want him to learn in a high and excited voice will make him pick up on it. Another great idea to get your bird to learn words is to play the radio and also cartoons to him. He will pick up on words that he hears often.

You will also notice your bird mumbling these words to himself before he actually says them out loud. This is his way of practicing what he has learnt. It seems like your bird is actually chattering to himself when he is learning words.

Chapter 6: Breeding Parakeets

When you buy a parakeet, it is a good idea to think about whether you want to breed them or not. If you can make up your mind initially, you can even buy your parakeets in pairs. That way, you can eliminate the process of introducing a mate to your parakeet.

That said, even if you decide to do so later on, you can follow a few simple rules and tips to make this phase a beautiful one. Parakeets breed readily in captivity. This is one of the reasons why there are so many hobby breeders. They also have interesting color mutations, which makes it even more challenging and exciting to breed them.

Parakeets become sexually mature at the age of about 2 years. It can be earlier or later depending upon each individual bird. However, 2 years is the right time to introduce a mate to your bird if you have decided to breed them.

1. Introducing a mate to your Parakeet

When you decide to introduce older birds to each other, the first thing to do is quarantine the new bird. Then, you must keep in mind that the female will be more aggressive and territorial than the male. These birds will dictate the whole relationship, the breeding season and also the rearing of the offspring.

So, if you have a female parakeet, the introduction must happen in a new and neutral environment where the female is less likely to be territorial. Follow the same steps mentioned in the earlier chapters about the introduction of two birds.

The next thing to do is to check whether the birds are showing any bonding behavior. The first sign is that the birds are feeding each other. If you do not see this behavior, you can give them wood that they can chew.

This is a part of the courtship ritual and you will eventually see them starting to feed one another. Only when you see this consistently should you provide a nesting box.

Never provide a nesting box before the birds have bonded. This will make the female hide in the nesting box all day and your birds will most likely not mate. Even if the birds do mate, the eggs that are laid are clear. They will not produce any chicks when they hatch.

Once the nesting box has been introduced after the birds have bonded, the male will initiate mating. During this phase you need to give the birds a larger portion of food. This will allow them to believe that they can provide for their young when they are born. Avoid touching the birds during this time. Also, avoid loud music or any other stressful conditions for the birds.

In the first few days of introduction, you need to watch the birds extremely carefully. If you see that one of them is excessively aggressive towards the other, they may not be a compatible pair. Simply separate the birds. In case you are providing the bird with any supplements, be very cautious. If one of them is getting an overdose of the supplement, he or she may become aggressive and hyperactive, leading you to believe that the birds are not compatible while they may actually be the perfect pair.

2. Preparing for the breeding season

All birds require a warm and comfortable nesting box in order to initiate mating. You also need to make sure that your birds get the right nutrition to ensure healthy offspring.

Setting up the nesting box

You need to get a large nesting box that is at least 18 inches deep or more. This is basically to make sure that plenty of the nesting material, usually something soft like pine shavings, is available. Parakeets tend to keep kicking this material out and if the nest is not deep enough, there are chances that the amount of pine shavings available will not be enough when the eggs are laid.

You can use a wooden nesting box. However, parakeets tend to be chewers and may damage the box. So a metal one is more suitable. The idea is to have a nesting box that can last for several breeding seasons. Parakeets prefer the same nesting box year after year.

This box can be placed at a high position in the cage. If you have a special nesting cage, you can place it there. Remember that height is an important factor for brooding hens to feel comfortable.

In case your bird does not have enough access to light, you may have to set up infrared lighting that you need to turn on at about 4pm and turn off by about 10pm.

The right diet for the breeding season

After mating, if the female spends most of her time in the nesting box, it only means that she is brooding. The diet of the brooding parakeets should be really nutritious to avoid common problems such as egg binding, which can be very painful and sometime fatal.

You need to give your parakeet fresh pellets, lots of fresh fruits and vegetables and even some cuttlebone to ensure that she has a good source of calcium. Ensuring that your parakeet is getting enough calcium can be a challenge but it is very important.

You can give them additional treats like raisins, almonds, walnuts, egg shells and even mineral blocks that are added to the water. Make sure that your bird gets good sunlight in order to utilize the calcium that you are providing her with.

Your vet should be able to help you with supplements that you can mix in the food or water of your parakeet.

Once the female has mated, she will begin to brood. You will know when she is ready to lay her eggs as she displays the following signs:

- Eating more from the mineral block or chewing from the cuttlebone.

- She will also become very cranky and noisy.

- Displaying territorial and aggressive behavior. The female will start seeking your attention and will want you to accept annoying behavior such as nipping at your shirt or biting. Do not encourage that.

- Development of a bald patch on the belly, which is called the brood patch. This is to help her pass heat from her body to the eggs.

When she is ready, she will lay the egg in the nesting box and will incubate it for about 28 days when provided with nesting conditions such as toys, sunlight and a lot of attention. Each clutch will have between 3 to 8 eggs. The hen lays one egg each day. It is possible that the first clutch is infertile. Parakeets are known for abandoning their clutch. If you see that your bird does not sit on the eggs and incubate them even after increasing the temperature, you will have to incubate the eggs artificially.

3. After the eggs have hatched

The biggest challenge that you will face is deciding between letting the birds parent the young ones or hand raising them yourself. If you allow the former, the baby birds will develop better parenting instincts that will help breed them in the future. In case of the latter, you will have birds that are friendlier and more accepting towards humans.

Most parakeet owners take the mid-road and co-parent the birds. This is ideal as the baby birds get the best of both worlds.

Hand raising parakeets

If you decide to hand feed the baby birds, the ideal age to remove them from the cage is when they are about 3-4 weeks old. This is when the birds are in their pinfeather stage. Their feathers look like quills at this stage.

This is the best age as the birds are able to hold the body heat and will not require any artificial heat. These birds also have the advantage of being raised by their parents and will be healthier. Immunity is better as the parents will pass on antibodies while feeding the babies.

Choose a formula recommended by your vet. Prepare the formula as per the instructions on the package. You need to make sure that the formula is heated to about 100 degrees F and not more than that. This can scald the insides of the delicate baby bird.

It is better to use a spoon to feed the baby as opposed to a syringe as you will be able to control the food going into the belly of the baby. That way you reduce the risk of choking the baby.

Feeding with a spoon is much slower. So chances of overfeeding are fewer. When the baby is full, you will be able to see the signs that will tell you when to stop feeding. You will also spend more time with the baby when you feed him with a spoon.

In case you pull the babies out of the nest earlier or have to hand feed them at an earlier stage because they were artificially incubated, you will have to purchase a brooder that will keep the babies warm as you feed them. The formula must be made very watery and should be given to the bird in small quantities. Then you wait for the crop to empty and feed the baby again. At a very young age, you may have to feed the baby every two hours.

In the case of the pinfeather stage, you can feed the baby 4-5 times and give him some time to rest overnight. That way the crop will be fully empty and he will be ready for next meal.

Co-parenting the baby birds

You may also choose to work with the parakeet parents and raise the chicks with them. This means that the parakeet parents will also be a part of the raising process. You will take turns between the feeding cycles and the babies will be removed from the nest to hand feed at least once a day.

Co-parenting is only possible when you have a very trusting relationship with your birds. If they can accept your attempts to take the babies out as assistance and not acceptance, then you can do this.

Your birds need to be extremely calm to allow you to co-parent the chicks. Otherwise they will develop aggressive behavior which they will direct at each other. The male may attack the female or they may even kill the hatchlings. You must back off if the birds show any signs of resistance.

However, if the birds accept your assistance, it can be a wonderfully rewarding experience for you. The responsibility is reduced on your part and on the part of the parakeet parents, the babies are more social and tame and the parents still have the pleasure of raising their own young.

It does not matter how you choose to raise the birds. Remember that all the experiences are equally rewarding. You may choose to add these birds to your flock. That is, however, not a practical thing to do as parakeets that have mated once will do so every year and the babies have a life span of about 30 years or more. So, it is a good idea to find these babies loving homes when they are a few years old.

Breeding parakeets is not for everyone. So make sure that you only do it if you are up for challenges such as the parents abandoning the young within a few days of the eggs hatching.

In case you find the first experience with the chicks less exciting, you can discourage breeding by not providing ideal nesting conditions as mentioned above. Some pet parakeet owners also avoid raising chicks because they find it very hard to give them away.

Weaning

During the hand feeding period, you will have to keep the birds in warm boxes or bins. When they are ready to be weaned, they are also ready for the cages. Until then, they are too small for a cage.

You know that the bird is ready to be weaned when he starts handling small objects with his beak or tries to climb using the beak. You will now reduce the formula to twice a day and introduce the bird to eating on his own. Weaning basically means that you are getting the bird to a stage when he can eat on his own without your help or the parent's help.

Place the babies in a cage that is lined with newspaper. Place a feeding bowl and a water bowl. You need one for each chick and it should be shallow enough for the bird to eat from. It is recommended that you put the bird into this cage after hand feeding in the morning. If the birds are very hungry, they may refuse to eat on their own.

You will be able to attract the babies to the new food, preferably special baby pellets, by mixing in rice crispies. You will see that they do not mind experimenting as long as their tummy isn't fully empty. Eventually, they will stop eating in the evening. Then they will slowly take to eating on their own and will wean with time. Never rush the baby. Prepare a feeding routine and stick to it and they will eventually learn to eat all their food on their own.

Chapter 7: Health of your Parakeet

The most important thing to keep in mind is to constantly monitor the health of your parakeet. When you are unable to identify the common illnesses in the initial stages, they manifest into something that can be potentially hazardous to your beloved bird.

Now, with most birds, it is very easy to identify when they are under the weather. They will display some very obvious changes in their behavior that you will be able to notice if you are a hands-on bird parent.

1. Identifying a Sick Parakeet

Many parakeet owners have spoken about unexpected deaths of their pets. While there are some diseases that have very low incubation periods, most can be detected quite easily at an early stage if the owner is able to recognize the signs of illness in the bird. This is what you need to watch out for:

- Resting too often
- Poor appetite
- Opening and closing the beak frequently
- Sticking to the bottom of the cage
- Reduced water intake or sudden increase in water intake
- Growth around the beak
- Loose droppings
- Sudden weight loss with the chest bone becoming more prominent
- Cloudy eyes
- Discharge from the eyes and nasal cavity
- Ruffled feathers
- Lethargy
- Drooping wings

2. Common Illnesses

For the most part, parakeets are hardy birds that are quite immune to most illnesses. However, there are a few infections and diseases that you need to know about as they commonly affect the parakeet as a species. We will talk about the identification, the cause and the cure for these conditions in the following section:

Proventricular Dilation Disease

This condition is also known as Parakeet Wasting Syndrome. In the past, this condition was considered to be fatal most of the time. However, new treatment methods have emerged over the years, which makes it possible to control the symptoms in the early stages.

This condition is caused by the Avian Bornavirus, which is believed to have spread rampantly due to the pet trade across the world. These viruses invade the cell of the host and continue to infect more cells eventually. The incubation period for this virus is about 4 weeks. It affects younger birds usually, although a parakeet is vulnerable at any age, especially during the breeding season. It can be spread from the hen to the eggs as well.

The common signs of PDD are:

- Poor digestion
- Traces of undigested foods in the feces
- Sudden increase or decrease in appetite
- Weight loss
- Depression
- Anorexia
- Lack of coordination
- Seizures
- Muscle deficiencies
- Feather plucking
- Constant crying or moaning

The treatment of this condition includes administration of anti-inflammatory drugs that can soothe the symptoms. However, the infection itself is seldom cured. Supplements like milk thistle and elemental formula for avians are also recommended.

Psittacine Beak and Feather Disease

With this condition, the cells of the feather and beak are killed by a strain of virus called the circovirus. This disease also impairs the immune system of the bird, leading to death of the bird from other infections in most cases.

This condition was first noticed among cockatoos but has affected several species of birds, mostly those belonging to the Psittacine family.

In most cases, death follows the infection. However, if the bird responds positively to the tests but has no signs of the diseases physically, it means that he or she is a carrier of the condition. This is when you have to quarantine the bird immediately. This is a contagious disease that spreads very easily.

The common signs of PBFD are:

- Abnormalities in the feathers
- Bumps and uneven edges in the beak
- Missing lumps of feathers
- Loss of appetite
- Diarrhea
- Regurgitation

In most cases, the birds will die before they show the above symptoms.

Treatment of the condition includes administering probiotics and mineral or vitamin supplementation. The only way to curb PBFD is to take preventive measures such as maintaining good sanitation and diet.

Psittacosis

This condition is also known as Chlamydiosis or Parrot Fever. The threat with this condition is that it can also affect human beings. It is a condition caused by a certain strain of bacteria called the Chlamydia Psittaci.

A few species of birds may never show symptoms of this condition and could be mere carriers. However, the fact that humans are susceptible to the condition requires you to take additional precautions.

This bacterial infection is only spread when you come in contact with the feces of the bird. This is true for other birds as well. So, maintaining good hygiene is the first step towards preventing this condition among the other birds in your aviary. You must also make sure that your birds are not exposed to the feces of wild birds when you let them out. The common problems leading to chlamydiosis are overcrowding of the aviary, improper quarantine measures etc.

The common signs of Chlamydiosis or Psittacosis are:
- Labored breathing
- Infection of the sinuses
- Runny nasal passage
- Discharge and swelling of the eyes
- Ruffled feathers
- Lethargy
- Dehydration
- Weight loss
- Abnormal droppings

These are the mild symptoms of the condition. In case of a chronic case of Psittacosis you will observe unusual positioning of the head, tremors, lack of co-ordination, paralysis of the legs and loss of control over the muscles.

The birds suspected with this condition are tested for a high WBC count and an increase in liver enzymes, which suggests liver damage. Antibiotics like Doxycycline and Tetracycline are usually administered to affected birds. In addition to that, supplements and medicated foods are also provided. However, because most birds refuse to eat when affected with this condition, it becomes a lot harder to give them proper treatment.

Aspergillosis

This is a condition that is non contagious but highly infectious. The fungus that causes this condition is known as Aspergillus Fumigatus and is known to be very opportunistic. That is why even the slightest signs of dampness will become breeding grounds for this fungi.

Young birds are mostly susceptible to this condition. In juvenile or baby birds, the rate of mortality is extremely high. Of course, in adult birds, they could become infected too. The spores of this fungus are easily inhaled, as they are extremely small. That is why, the infection is mostly seen in the air capillaries of the affected bird.

The most common signs of aspergillosis include:

- Polydipsia or abnormal thirst
- Stunted growth
- Lethargy
- Ruffled feathers
- Anorexia
- Polyuria or large amounts of urine in the excreta
- Wheezing
- Coughing
- Nasal Discharge
- Tremors
- Ataxia or loss of control over the limbs
- Cloudy eyes

This condition mainly affects the respiratory tract. However, other organs may also be affected in some rare cases of infection. Treatment of this condition is challenging because of the loss of immunity in birds. So the affected bird could also have multiple infections caused by other microorganisms. Normally, systemic antifungal therapy is recommended. The lesions caused at the site of infection may also be removed through suction or surgery.

Preventive care is the best way to keep your bird safe. Maintaining a high standard of husbandry will help you control infections by depriving the fungus of any breeding sites.

Avian sinusitis

It is quite common for the sinuses of the birds to get infected. This condition is mostly associated with a deficiency in Vitamin A. This leads to abnormal cell division that will be seen in the form of thickened mucus around the eyes. This can further lead to abscesses or conjunctivitis is the affected bird. There are debates about the causal factor, however.

The earliest signs of this condition are:
- Clicking
- Proptosis or protrusion of the eyeball
- Sneezing
- Excessive secretion of mucus

Later on, you will notice that there is swelling around the eyes as well as the region around the beak of the bird. When the sinus is infected, it is also possible for the bird to be suffering from associated conditions such as pneumonia.

A needle biopsy of the area with swelling helps diagnose the condition. This helps you differentiate the condition form abscesses that require a completely different treatment altogether.

The bird is treated with an antibiotic called Baytril that can curb any infection by bacteria such as pseudomonas. In addition to this, the bird also requires Vitamin A supplementation which may be administered through an intramuscular injection. The sinus is flushed if the swelling is too much.

You must also improve the diet of the bird and include as many dark green vegetables as possible. Oranges are also recommended to improve the condition. Lastly, you need to include only fortified pellets in your bird's diet to help restore the Vitamin A levels in the body.

Psittacine Herpes Virus

Also known as Pacheco's disease, this condition was first recognized in the country of Brazil. Aviculturists observed that birds began to die within a few days of being unwell. In less than 3-4 days, a herpes virus infection will cause nasal discharge and abnormal feces. This condition is very contagious and is often fatal.

Parakeets are highly susceptible to this condition. This condition is generally transmitted through the feces or the nasal discharge. The problem with this virus is that it remains stable even outside the body of the host.

It will be seen on different surfaces in the cage, the food and the water bowls. As a result, it spreads quite easily. Of course, there are possibilities of transmission of this condition from the mother to the embryo.

In many cases, a bird could be a mere carrier of the condition without any symptoms. A bird that has survived an infection is a potential threat to your flock.

The symptoms of this condition commonly include:
- Ruffled Feathers
- Diarrhea
- Sinusitis
- Anorexia
- Conjunctivitis
- Tremors in the neck, legs and wings
- Lethargy
- Weight loss
- Green colored feces

In most cases, death occurs due to enlargement in the liver or the spleen. When subjected to stress and sudden climate changes, the virus can get activated in birds that are carriers, leading to their death.

A PCR test is conducted to screen the birds for a herpes virus infection. In some cases, a bird that is tested positive could show no symptoms at all.

There is no known cure for this condition. Only preventive measures can be taken by keeping the cage conditions pristine. You also need to ensure that your bird does not undergo any stress or trauma. When he is not well exercised or mentally stimulated, there are chances of activation of this strain of virus.

Coacal papillomas

This is yet another condition that is said to be caused by a strain of virus called Papillomavirus. This condition leads to benign tumors in the regions of the bird's body that are unfeathered. There are a few debates about the causal factors of this condition, however. This is because of the internal lesions detected with this condition that is caused by a strain of Herpes virus.

Common symptoms of the condition include:

- Wart like growths on the legs and feet
- Loose droppings
- Dried fecal matter around the vent area
- Blood in the droppings of the bird

In case you suspect this condition in your parakeet, you can make a preemptive diagnosis at home. Apply a small amount of 5% acetic acid on the cloacal region. If this turns white, then your bird is probably infected.

Proper diagnosis includes a biopsy of the tissue that is affected. The growth on the legs and feet will be removed surgically as the first step to treatment. This condition leads to a compromised immune system that can further lead to secondary infections by bacteria and other microorganisms.

If your bird harbors any internal papillomas, you need to have them monitored frequently for any infection in the GI tract. If left ignored, it can lead to tumors in the bile duct or the pancreas.

Kidney dysfunction

There are two kinds of kidney dysfunction that you can observe in your bird:

Chronic renal failure: This is when the kidney becomes progressively dysfunctional. At the onset, the bird will show very few signs and will only seem mildly under the weather.

Acute renal failure: This is when both the kidneys fail and deteriorate rapidly. The condition is usually reversible but the kidneys will be compromised to a great extent.

How to tell if your bird has developed any of these kidney diseases:
- Polydipsia, or excessive water consumption, followed by frequent urination is common. This is the bird's attempt to flush out toxins from the blood as the kidney is unable to perform this function effectively.
- Watery droppings
- Enlargement of the abdomen
- Constipation
- Vomiting
- Inability to fly
- Fluffing of feathers
- Depression
- Lethargy
- Weakness
- Blood in the droppings
- Dehydration
- Swollen joints
- Inability to walk or balance himself

These renal diseases can be caused by microbial infections. The common virus responsible for this condition is the Polyomavirus, while the most common fungus seen is the Aspergillus fungi.

There are various other causes like excessive vitamin D consumption, allergy to any antibiotics or medication that has been administered, heavy metal poisoning, toxicity by pesticides and ingestion of certain plants.

Gout, which is the inability of the bird to release waste from the body, also leads to kidney failure over time.

Proper diagnosis of this condition requires a full medical history of the bird. This is followed by a physical examination, blood chemistry tests, blood count tests and a urine analysis. In ambiguous cases, cloacal swabs, endoscopy and ultrasound are used to confirm the condition that the bird has been affected with.

Supportive care, including tube feeding and providing the right supplements, aids recovery of the bird. It is recommended that the blood of the bird be tested on a regular basis to change the treatment method as required by the body of the bird.

Antibiotics may be administered, as bacteria is the common cause of renal failure in birds. There could also be some secondary infections that need to be treated with antibiotics. Besides this, depending upon the nature of the infection, antifungal and antiviral medicines are provided.

In the case of toxicity or gout, vitamin A supplementation is encouraged. There could also be surgical intervention if tumors or lesions are detected internally.

It is recommended that you include proteins, Vitamin B complex, Vitamin C and Vitamin A in the diet of the bird. Foods like dandelion root, cranberry, parsley and nettle tea will help improve the functioning of the kidneys and will aid in quick recovery of the affected bird.

Lipomas or Tumors

It is possible for pet birds to develop tumors or lipomas on their bodies. These are usually seen as bumps or lumps on the skin or just under the skin. Of course, every lump is not an indication of tumor as some of them could also be abscesses.

In many cases, what is feared to be a tumor could be a cyst that is covered with fluids or pus. These are not cancerous and will not spread like the tumors.

A tumor is a solid tissue mass that can grow very quickly and spread across the body of the bird. It can occur in any part of the body and need immediate attention to ensure that your bird is able to recover from it.

There are two kinds of tumors: Benign and malignant. The benign tumors do not cause cancer while the malignant ones are cancerous. While both can adversely affect the health of the bird, benign tumors are less urgent than the malignant ones.

The reason for this is that the benign tumors do not spread to other parts of the bird's body like the malignant ones. There are chances of growth in this tumor but they almost never spread. Even if they do, there is enough time to provide medical care effectively.

That does not mean that you can ignore these tumors. They need to be removed at the earliest. Since they get bigger in size, they can put a lot of pressure on the internal organs of the bird, leading to severe discomfort and even damage.

Malignant tumors will damage the nearby tissues of the affected organ as well. A process called metastasis is responsible for this. This is when the cell breaks away from the tumor and travels through the blood stream. Then it spreads to various parts of the body to cause multiple tumors.

Usually a tumor is caused by mutations in the DNA of the bird's cells. Normal cells will not divide uncontrollably like the tumors. They multiply enough to grow and repair the body.

There are several other factors like the environment of the bird, inclusion of carcinogens in the diet of the bird, nutritional deficiencies, old age and interbreeding that compromises the immune system of the bird, leading to this condition.

There are various types of tumors that can affect a bird. The most common one is that of the skin or the squamous cells of the skin. This leads to tumors near the eyes, around the preen gland, on the skin on the head and around the beak. A huge causal factor for this is self-mutilation by the birds. This is an external tumor that you can identify as lumps on the surface of the skin.

Another type of tumor that affects birds is a fibroid tumor. This affects the connective tissues of the bird. Usually, these tumors are benign. When they become malignant, the condition is known as fibrosarcoma. These tumors are also external and will be seen on the legs, wings, the beak and the sternum of the bird.

The most common type of internal tumor is a tumor in the reproductive organs or the kidneys. Again, these tumors could either be malignant or benign. The problem with these internal tumors is that they will go unnoticed until the bird falls severely sick. The pressure of these tumors on the internal organs leads to a lot of discomfort and stress for the birds. In most cases, the digestive system experiences a lot of stress, leading to improper digestion of food. The droppings are not excreted effectively from the body either. It can also put a lot of pressure on the nervous system, making the bird uncoordinated.

Birds can also develop cancers in the lymphatic system. This compromises the immune system to a large extent, leading to secondary bacterial, viral or fungal infections. When the tumor is malignant, the condition is known as lymphoma. It is characterized by swollen lymph nodes in most cases.

Another type of tumor in the birds are lipomas. These are made mostly of mature fat cells. You will find these tumors just under the skin of the bird near the abdomen and he chest. They interfere with the body movements and will also lead to lethargy and inactivity. These are normally seen in obese birds.

Tumors that are external are easily identified as they appear in the form of lumps. Any abnormal growth on the body should be shown to the vet immediately. A pathologist will examine samples from the affected area and will determine if it is a tumor or not. The next step is to check if it is malignant or benign.

The internal tumors are really hard to detect. You will notice symptoms like:
- Loss of weight
- Increased sleep
- Loss of appetite
- Inability to balance the body

- Lameness

These symptoms could be indicative of any other disease as well. So, you need to have your bird checked by a vet the moment you notice them.

Treatment of tumors or lipomas includes surgical removal of the mass of cells. If the tumor is growing or changing and is located in a part of the body that can affect its daily activities, surgery is preferred.

Prognosis of benign tumors is definitely better than the malignant ones. It could just require removal of the tissue in most cases.

It is the malignant tumors that are harder to treat. This is because they may continue to spread even after removal, unless they are removed at a very early stage.

Tumors of the kidney, the liver and other vital organs are the hardest to deal with as they could lead to death of the bird during surgery due to excessive bleeding.

In the case of parakeets, it is a lot easier thanks to the size of the birds. The larger the animal, the easier it is to carry out surgical processes.

In rare cases, radiation and chemotherapy may help control these malignant tumors. They will be used in conjunction to surgical processes.

This is a very recent practice in avian medicine. That is why most avian vets will have less experience with providing radiation to birds. However, when there are very few avenues of treatment, radiation may be used on an experimental basis.

The drugs used in chemotherapy are very harsh. Since birds are easily susceptible to toxicity, there are chances that the bird dies of poisoning in the course of this treatment.

If the tumor is malignant, there is very little chance of survival unless the bird is treated in the initial stages. That is why it is recommended to take your bird for regular check-ups by the veterinarian. That way the tests will be able to detect internal tumors, if any.

Toxicity

Heavy metal poisoning due to metals like zinc and lead is quite common in pet birds. This is because of the several sources of toxicity that we neglect while getting the house bird proofed.

Zinc poisoning:

The discomfort caused depends upon the amount of toxins that are present in the body of the bird. There are some signs of toxicity that you need to watch out for:
- Shallow breathing
- Lethargy
- Anorexia
- Weight loss
- Weakness
- Kidney dysfunction
- Blue or purple coloration of the skin
- Feather picking
- Regurgitation
- Paleness in the mucous membrane
- Excessive consumption of water followed by urination to flush the toxins out
- Inability to balance the body

The most common sources of infection are the cages, toys and wires around the cage that are galvanized, washers or nuts made from zinc and pennies that were minted after the year 1983.

Lead poisoning:

Lead poisoning is more fatal as the lead that is absorbed will be retained in the soft tissues of the body. This can cause neural damage and can even lead to problems with the kidneys and the GI system.

The symptoms of lead poisoning are the same as zinc poisoning. But the sources of zinc poisoning are a lot more abundant in comparison. The common sources are tooth brushes, lead paint, lead weights used for curtains, crystal, cardboard boxes, dyes used in newspapers, vinyl or plastic material, stainless glass windows, plumbing material, foils of some champagne bottles etc.

To treat this condition, an injection called Calsenate is administered. This acts like an antidote that will remove the zinc or lead that has entered the body. If the bird has ingested any metal object, it can be removed surgically. The bird must be put on a recommended diet to ensure that the kidneys and the liver do not shut down, making it harder for the metals to be eliminated from the body.

Make sure that your bird is in a safe environment in order to prevent any metal poisoning. If you are unsure of how to do this on your own, you have several professionals who can come to your home and take care of the whole bird proofing process for you.

Feather plucking

This is often considered a behavioral disorder but can also be associated with several physiological conditions that cause extreme discomfort to the bird.

Feather plucking is a form of self-mutilation where the bird plucks the skin off his body, leading to large bald patches and also infections due to the wounds caused by plucking. The causes for feather plucking are many, including:

- **Malnutrition:** When major nutrients like magnesium and calcium are absent from the bird's diet, it can lead to irritation of the skin, forcing the bird to pluck at the feathers.

- **Allergies:** If your bird is allergic to any foods or preservatives, he may resort to feather plucking.

- **Boredom:** When parakeets do not get the necessary amount of exercise and mental stimulation, they get extremely bored and will choose feather plucking as a form of entertainment.

- **Light:** Parakeets require a good amount of sunlight. If you keep the cage in a dark corner of your home, the bird will develop Vitamin D deficiency, which makes him vulnerable to feather plucking. You can see a complete change in the way your bird behaves with a simple change in the availability of natural light.

One medicine that is effective in controlling the condition is Clomipramine, which helps in the regrowth of feathers. The inflammation in the affected areas is also reduced, making the bird reduce the action of plucking feathers.

In case of stress induced feather plucking, it is possible to treat the condition effectively with antidepressants, hypnotics and sedatives. This is required if you travel with the bird, introduce another bird or make changes in the routine of the bird. Any form of change in the immediate environment or shock can make your bird vulnerable to feather plucking.

It is important for you to spend as much time with your bird as possible. Feather clipping is a great measure to prevent escapes or flight related injuries. However, it is a rather big setback for the bird. Flying is the best form of exercise for the bird and also keeps him entertained. Of course a housing area that is too small for the bird to fly is also a bad idea.

You need to make sure that your parakeet is stimulated mentally as well. This includes buying him a lot of toys or even providing him with homemade foraging toys that keep him engaged.

Spending time with your bird can act as the best measure against feather plucking in most cases. Train the bird, play with him or simply talk to him for a few minutes. These birds are extremely social and a lack of bonding with a mate or the flock will make them behave differently.

If everything fails, you need to make sure that your bird is checked by a vet for any other internal conditions or infections. In this case, feather plucking is merely a symptom and not a behavioral condition. It can be controlled by treating the causal health problem.

3. Accidents and Injuries

Accidents are very common with birds, especially when they are able to fly. There could be additional problems like fights within the flock, sudden aggression due to breeding seasons, feather clipping accidents or poisoning that require immediate attention.

These emergencies require you to provide the right type of first aid in order to prevent any untoward effects on the bird. There are a few common problems that you may have to face when you have a bird at home:

Broken blood feathers

When the blood feather is broken, a lot of blood is lost. This is not a cause for concern as long as the bird is given the right treatment to prevent bleeding. The best thing to do would be to apply light pressure on the affected area and apply some flour on the area. You can keep it covered with gauze until you reach the veterinarian. In most cases, the blood feather will be pulled out.

Wounds and abrasions

Birds may have some wounds on the surface of the skin. Normally wounds and abrasions are superficial and can be managed with some simple cleaning with hydrogen peroxide or betadine. If there is any dirt on the wound, you can get rid of it with a pair of tweezers. Then, you may apply some antibiotic ointment as a preventive measure. Make sure that the bird does not pick on the wound. If it is deep and has exposed the flesh, you need to see a veterinarian immediately.

Attacks by dogs or cats

Parakeets are large birds. However, they are also easily stressed when an animal like a dog goes after them. If this happens, you need to remain extremely calm and keep the bird in a quiet place to prevent further stress.

The next thing to do would be to check for the damage on the body. In case of any broken wings or bones, all you need to do is tie it to the body of the bird with gauze lightly. This will prevent any movement and further damage. In case of any damage to the skull or the legs, you will have to call your veterinarian home.

Cat and dog saliva can be toxic for birds. Therefore, it is a must that you have the bird checked, even if the injuries are minute. This prevents any chances of bacterial infections or other infections.

Tongue bleeding

The tongue of a bird has several blood vessels and can be damaged, sometimes due to toys or even while climbing. You will notice that the tongue bleeds quite profusely. So you will have to make sure that you see a vet immediately. You cannot use a styptic pencil in this case. Even flour can choke the bird.

Bleeding toenails

This is quite common, as birds can have their toenails stuck in upholstery or on your shirt and just rip them off when they are trying to fly away. This is not a very serious condition as it can be managed with a simple dab of the styptic pencil. It is when the bleeding is unstoppable that you should take the bird to the vet immediately.

Labored breathing

If your bird is experiencing any shortness of breath or is wheezing while inhaling, it is a sign of some form of nasal blockage.

The first thing you need to do is check if there are any blockages in the nasal passage. In case of any dried mucus, you can just wipe it off with a wet cloth. Other obstructions include seeds or parts of toys. Do not try to remove it yourself if you notice it as you may harm the bird. Take him to a vet immediately.

Open mouth breathing or panting can be caused by overheating of the body. This could be because of travelling, exercise or even a change in the temperature. If this is ignored, the bird may have a heat stroke. You will notice that the bird will stretch its wings out, breathe very heavily and just collapse in the case of a heatstroke.

In this case, the bird must immediately be shifted to a cooler place. Hold a cold towel around the body of the bird. If the bird is able to stand, you can even get him to stand in a shallow bowl of cold water.

Shortness of breath could be an indication of several other diseases. Therefore, make sure you consult your vet immediately.

Burns

If the bird lands on a hot stove or a hot pan, he can have severe burns. Sometimes even the radiator can lead to burns. You need to make sure that the affected area is washed immediately with cold water. Then, using clean gauze, wipe the area dry gently. A cold compress is the best remedy for mild burns.

In case of any severe burns, you will have to take your bird to the emergency room or consult your vet immediately. These birds tend to go into extreme shock and will need care immediately. Most often, besides the topical treatment, antibiotics are administered to prevent any infections of the wounds.

Chilling

Birds like the parakeet are from the tropics and will not be able to handle very cold temperatures. It is mandatory to keep them in a warm area. Sometimes, you may even have to use a heat lamp to keep the temperatures up.

If your bird is suffering from chilling, you will have to supply heat to the body with a warm towel or even a heat lamp that is set to about 90 degrees Fahrenheit. Chilling can be caused by shock or injury and it requires immediate medical attention in that case. Environmental changes, drafts and even very cold air conditioning can lead to chilling.

Preparing a first aid kit

A first aid kit is a must in a home with any pets. You need to prepare a first aid kit that can help you to provide emergency care to the bird when required. The items you need to include are:

- The number and directions to your veterinary clinic or the emergency facility suggested by your avian vet.
- Phone numbers for poison control. You will be able to get this information from your vet.
- Scissors in order to remove any strings or to cut bandaging material.
- Sterilized gauze
- Q-tips to clean up a wound and to apply any topical medicine.
- Tape
- A roll of clean gauze to wrap a wing that is injured.
- Antibiotic cream recommended by the vet.
- Styptic pencil to control bleeding.
- Betadine or Hydrogen Peroxide to clean any wound.
- Pliers or tweezers to handle small bandages and tapes.
- Heating pad to help a bird experiencing chilling.
- An ink dropper to administer internal medication.
- Large towels to handle the bird.
- Thermometer to measure the temperature of the bird's body.

Keep all of the above in a box that is easily accessible and make sure that your family is aware of the different situations that may require the first aid kit. They also need to be told how the bird can be helped in case of common accidents and injuries around the house.

4. Preventive Measures

Prevention is always better than cure. It is really heartbreaking to see your beloved pet wallow in pain and die an unexpected death. Instead of multiple veterinary meetings, it is a good idea to take a few simple preventive measures to keep your birds safe:

• **Keep them away from wild birds or animals:** The cage should be kept in an area that is not accessible to any wild birds or rodents like mice that generally carry a lot of disease causing microbes. The food and water should not be contaminated. Any spilled food or litter should be cleaned up immediately to make sure that these creatures are not attracted.

• **Clean up as much as you can:** The housing area of the bird must be pristine. The most common breeding grounds for bacteria, parasites and viruses include organic matter in the cage such as the feces.

Make sure that the cage is cleaned on a regular basis. You need to be additionally cautious if you are planning to keep the birds outdoors.

You must make it a rule not to borrow equipment or allow other bird owners to handle your parakeet. This can lead to the transmission of unwanted feather dander or microbe carrying debris.

• **Keep an eye on your bird:** Be an attentive bird parent. If your parakeet shows the slightest deviation from what you consider normal, become alert. You may have to take your bird to the vet to have him examined completely. It may seem like you are too overprotective at times. However, it is necessary that you catch any disease as early as you can to provide suitable treatment to help the bird cope with it and recover fast.

• **Follow good quarantining:** Make sure that any new bird that is included in the flock is quarantined properly. Most often, a bird could simply be a carrier of the condition. When kept in quarantine, you will be able to observe the bird for any abnormality. This can be treated effectively before it spreads to other birds in your household. Even if you plan to take your bird to shows or exhibitions, you will have to quarantine him for at least two weeks before reintroducing him to the flock. A great way to ensure that your bird is not a carrier is to find a good breeder who practices strict disease control at his center.

• **Regular vet visits:** Your bird needs to be checked regularly for any chance of infections. Make sure that you never miss your annual veterinary checkup if you want to keep your bird in good health at all times. Here are a few recommended tests that you should have the vet conduct to be sure that your bird is free from deadly diseases:

Adult birds:
- Complete blood count to make sure that there are no internal infection.
- Study of culture to diagnose any possibility of yeast or bacterial infection.
- Full body X-ray.

Young birds:
- Complete blood count to check for any internal infection.
- Chlamydophilia Immunoassay in order to diagnose parrot fever that is highly contagious, affecting birds and human beings.
- Culture study to eliminate chances of yeast or bacterial infections.

You can never be too sure of the right methods to take good care of your bird. However, you can be a good parent by eliminating all the chances of the disease and reduce the risk for your beloved parakeet. With these preventive measures you can take care of most deadly conditions easily.

5. Finding the perfect avian vet

Birds are extremely different from other pets. The anatomy and the basic requirements of these creatures are very different. So, you need to have a certified avian vet who can help your bird.

Avian vets have a degree in veterinary medicine but have dedicated a large portion of their practice to birds. Every country has an association that vets can register under to stay updated about this science. One such association is the Association of Avian Vets or AAV. You can find all the registered avian vets in your vicinity using their official website which is www.aav.org.

If you are unable to find a good avian vet on this website, you have the option of asking a regular vet for leads. You may also contact parakeet clubs in your city for more information.

When you are choosing an avian vet, here are a few things that you need to look for:

- Staff that are trained to handle birds. They will be comfortable around your birds and will know a little bit about the species as well.
- There should be an emergency facility linked with the clinic in case your bird needs immediate attention. It is best to look for a clinic that even has a pet hospital for in house patients.
- The vet should have mostly avian patients. If he is only seeing one or two birds in a day, he is most likely not an avian vet. Some of the avian vets also deal with exotic pets like reptiles but will dedicate most of their practice to birds.
- Each examination should be for at least 30 minutes. If the interval between each patient is just about 15 minutes, your bird may not be getting a thorough examination.
- The clinic should be as close to your home as possible. Drives are extremely stressful for pets and should be minimal.

Your avian vet should also be updated with the facilities available for birds. If he is part of the AAV or attends regular seminars about avian medicine, you can be sure that your bird is in great hands.

6. Insuring Parakeets

When you approach a vet for your parakeet, you can even ask about the insurance policies available for pet birds. Some of them will cover most medical expenses in case of an emergency and will also be able to provide third party liability in case of any damage caused by your bird to another person's property. Your vet will be associated with certain health insurance companies that can help you take care of all the medical expenses with respect to your bird.

Usually, these insurance policies have a premium of $100-250 or £50-100 depending upon the cover that you are looking at. However, they are worth the investment as you will be able to get a lot of support when your bird requires any emergency care or assistance. Last minute expenses can be very stressful if your bird does not have insurance. In addition to that, insurance will come in very handy when you are travelling with your bird. Most airlines insist that your bird be insured before taking them on board. For the medical expenses, you also have the option of opening a savings account that you can set aside some money in on a monthly basis to help in case of an emergency.

Conclusion

Thank you for putting your faith in this book. Hopefully, all your queries about handling a parakeet have been answered effectively. As you bond with your bird and learn more about him, your knowledge will automatically see a surge. Until then, this book is meant to serve as the first step towards learning about bird care.

Since the book is based on experiences of other parakeet owners, you can be certain that all the information is authentic and practical. That way, you will be able to identify the problem easily and apply the suggested solution.

If this book has helped you make a decision about purchasing the bird, then my work is done. Whether you decided to go for a parakeet or not, you have made a good choice. If you are honestly unable to take care of the bird, then it is best to avoid stress to the bird as well as yourself.

However, if you did choose to bring a bird home, you must know that your life has changed forever. You will find the best companion in your parakeet. These birds are extremely loving and affectionate and are worth all the efforts you put in.

References

Note: at the time of printing, all the websites below were working. As the Internet changes rapidly, some sites might no longer be live when you read this book. That is, of course, out of our control.

The more you update your knowledge about your pet bird, the better your journey with him will be. Here are some of the best online resources that you can turn to in order to get all the information that you need about these birds:

www.cuteness.com
www.budgerigarparakeets.com
www.parakeetsecrets.com
www.pets.thenest.com
www.budgerigar.com
www.thesprucepets.com
www.invasives.org.za
www.talkbudgies.com
www.parakeetforum.com
www.budgiekeet.com
www.budgieplace.com
www.theparrotclub.co.uk
www.avianandexotic.com
www.budgie-info.com
www.repticzone.com
www.goodbirdinc.com
www.theparakeetperch.com
www.sallybudgie.blogspot.com
www.incrediblebudgerigar.blogspot.com
www.alankentbudgerigars.com
www.timfoddybudgerigars.co.uk
www.concordvets.com.au
www.windycityparrot.com
www.caminoanimalclinic.com
www.birdcagesnow.com
www.birdwatchingblog.us
www.beautyofbirds.com
www.petsuppliesplus.com
www.oldworldaviaries.com
www.parrotsecrets.com

Published by Zoodoo Publishing 2018

CPSIA information can be obtained
at www.ICGtesting.com
Printed in the USA
LVOW13s1049260718

584996LV00006BA/180/P